# Prayer—The Heartbeat of the Church

# Prayer—The Heartbeat of the Church

## By P. Douglas Small

Library of Congress Catalog Card Number: 2008935529
ISBN: 978-1-59684-396-7
Copyright © 2008 by Pathway Press
Cleveland, Tennessee 37311
All Rights Reserved
Printed in the United States of America

# DEDICATION

To the late *S. A. Lankford, Walter Barwick,*
*C. L. Leonard,* and *Henry Smith*—pastors in my
"growing-up" years.

To the memory of the *cottage prayer meetings* and
the *Sunday nights intercession in the prayer room* fueling
the Sunday night services. To the *saints* expending
their energy for those pre-service prayer times with
tear-stained faces and joyful shouts.

To the unforgettable experience of *seeing*
*grown men* with their knees planted on bare concrete,
praying over wellworn, marked-up Bibles lying
open on cane-backed chairs, passionately *praying as*
*if they were preaching.*

To the *Norwood, North Carolina, Church of God*—a
praying church—that nurtured me as a boy.

"Do not pray for easy lives. Pray to be stronger men. Do not pray for tasks equal to your powers. Pray for powers equal to your tasks. Then the doing of your work shall be no miracle, but you shall be the miracle" (Phillips Brooks,1835-1893).

# CONTENTS

## Covenant
## Prayer—The Heartbeat
### of the Church

We believe that God has divinely commissioned the Church of God to be a champion for truth in the twenty-first century.

We believe He has instituted prayer as a direct source of power from Him to embrace the mandate to effectively expand His kingdom and to live the abundant life in Jesus Christ.

We will therefore . . .

**Make** *prayer a priority in fulfilling the mission and vision of the Church of God.*

**Recognize** *that prayer is the direct channel to connect with the presence, promises, and power of God.*

**Endorse** *the outlined prayer initiative as set forth by the leadership of the Church of God.*

**Participate** *in Great Days of Prayer, churchwide Prayer Study, and Wednesday Morning Prayer time.*

We embrace these covenant statements with our hearts and confess them with our mouths, and boldly stand on the eternal truths of God's unchanging Word to fulfill them. Be it so!

AMEN!

# FOREWORD

In the book *Leadership That Works*, Dr. Leith Anderson recounts the true story of a denomination that found itself in serious decline. The denominational leaders called on a church-consulting firm to assess the problem and prescribe a cure. After months of study, research, and interviews, the consultants met with church leaders. The denomination was told it was too far gone. Nothing substantive could be done to reverse the decline.

Sitting in stunned silence, the leaders were motionless. Finally, one of them broke the silence: "Are you telling us there is *nothing* we can do?" "Well," came the response, "you can pray." Hearing that verdict, the leader fell to his knees and began to pray. The responsibility touched everyone in the room, and they prayed through their lunch hour and into the afternoon. They began meeting together regularly to pray. They called their people to prayer. God heard their prayers, arrested the decline, and today that group is moving forward.

Prayer is the rhythmic and perpetual heartbeat of the body of Christ. It sustains and energizes the Church, providing fervency for worship, strength and energy for serving, and motivation for action. It is an indispensable lifeline to the resources of heaven. Prayer must be our most strategic action if we are to have spiritual renewal. History proves the power of prayer.

Dr. Charles W. Conn references prayer, seeking God, and supplication at least forty-three times in his first five chapters of the Church of God history, *Like a Mighty Army*. We read comments like these: "They spent much time in prayer, praying into the night," and "They were praying and weeping constantly."

Our Pentecostal roots grow deeply into the soil of prayer. Prayer stabilized our infancy. Prayer gave victory in the face of persecution. Prayer sustained balance amid fanaticism. Prayer strengthened us through decades of cultural change and satanic attacks. Prayer is the heartbeat of the Church. This is why the Bible enjoins us to . . .

- "Seek the Lord and His strength; seek His face evermore" (1 Chron. 16:11).
- "Ask . . . seek . . . knock" (Matt. 7:7).
- "Watch therefore, and pray always" (Luke 21:36).
- "[Pray] always with all prayer and supplication in the Spirit . . . for all the saints" (Eph. 6:18).
- "Continue earnestly in prayer, being vigilant" (Col. 4:2).
- "Pray without ceasing" (1 Thess. 5:17).
- "The harvest truly is plentiful, but the laborers are few. Therefore pray the Lord of the harvest to send out laborers into His harvest" (Matt. 9:37-38).

Prayer is the holy and intimate intersection of God and His church, where He delegates authority to His church to enforce His will on earth as it is in heaven. Prayer is more than presentation; it is partnership. It is more than exercise; it is enforcement. It is more than activity; it is authority. Prayer is our mission because praying is our ministry. If we are to evangelize, plant churches, disciple believers, raise up leaders, and preach the Gospel, we must pray. Let us teach prayer and preach prayer; but most of all, let us pray. Our mission is our ministry. As we pray, we will prevail.

RAYMOND F. CULPEPPER
*General Overseer*
*Church of God*

# INTRODUCTION

The Church of God has always been a church of prayer. Prayer laid the foundation for the movement, and has guided us in remarkable worldwide ministry and growth. This volume emphasizes the biblical truth that prayer *is* the heartbeat of the Church. It is the vital element in going "Forward Together in Prayer."

## PRAYER INITIATIVE: MISSION

To send forth a Spirit-directed call for the entire Church of God family to unite in prayer for worship renewal and intensity, discipleship growth and maturity, and passionate outreach.

## PRAYER INITIATIVE: MATERIALS

Priority attention has been given to developing support materials for making *Prayer—The Heartbeat of the Church* effective and impactful. These items will help create a sustained prayer culture in the Church.

1. *Study Book*—a copy for each church family

2. *Instructors Guide*—a copy for church leaders

3. *DVD*—a copy for the church. It contains six lessons to begin the study of each chapter.

4. *Resource Guide*—a copy for prayer leaders

5. *40-Day Devotional Guide*—a copy for each church member. It contains a devotion for each day while the book is being read or taught.

6. *Prayer Reminder Card*—a card for each church member. The wallet/purse card prompts us "to pray always" and "to expect positive results."

7. *Sermon Seeds*—a set for the pastor.

All support materials can be ordered from Pathway Press at *1-800-553-8506.*

## Prayer Initiative: METHODS

The heartbeat of the Church is to create a prayer culture and to get every member involved in a consistent prayer life. This book can construct a foundation for this to happen. Here are some ways to teach this material:

1. **Utilize** six Sunday evenings to teach the course and to sponsor a time of united prayer.

2. **Designate** a series of Wednesday evenings to sponsor the prayer initiative: teach, discuss, pray.

3. **Organize** several prayer strategies while the book is being taught—prayer walks, home prayer groups, a prayer breakfast, and so forth.

4. **Promote** the prayer initiative by utilizing different media venues—church bulletin, direct mail, telephone calls, pulpit announcements.

## Prayer of Consecration

*Father, You have invited us to purifying, uplifting, and fortifying communion with You. You have promised that if we "ask, seek, and knock" through prayer, we will receive, find, and experience. Guide us as we study* Prayer–The Heartbeat of the Church, *and come together in prayer. Make us one in unity, faith, and love, as we create a culture of prayer in our church.*

# CHAPTER 1

# Understanding Prayer

**Foundation Study:** God's Pursuit of Man

**Bible Focus:** Gen. 1:28; 2:15-17; 3:8-19

## Central Truth

The first encounters between God and man are in Genesis 1, 2, and 3. In each case God takes the initiative. His first message is a blessing to and through man (1:28-29). The second encounter is a gracious warning (2:16-17). Heightened sensitivity should also come through prayer. The third encounter is God's redemptive response to the fall of man (3:9-19). Prayer, then, appropriates God's blessings. To be effective, it must hear and heed God's warnings of perils and dangers that deny His purposes and cause us to forfeit both blessings and our strategic role. It redeems mistakes and renews our relationship with God.

## Key Principles

Biblical scholars speak of the "law of the first mention." On any subject in Scripture, they look for added significance, for implications that give clues to the importance of some person, place, or thing. Since the essence of prayer is an encounter with God and the context in which God engages us, the law of the first mention would see Him as the great and gracious initiator. Through prayer, He blesses (Gen. 1:28), sets boundaries (2:17), and redemptively pursues us (3:8ff.). He will not let us hide from Him, ourselves, or one another.

## Points of Emphasis

1. God's first words to man are in the form of a blessing (Gen. 1:28). What blessings are you missing because of missed time with God?

2. Prayer is the means by which God decrees our productivity, not merely at the level of *addition*, but at the level of *multiplication*. God doesn't add; He multiplies.

3. Prayer is the means by which God empowers man, giving him dominion. It is the gateway to victory, to an overcoming posture in life. God offers us the kingly status of governance as we pray. It is not His intention that we face life on earth as victims, but as victors.

4. In prayer, God gave freely to Adam all that was in the garden. Is this benevolent, giving God the One to whom you pray? Or do you see Him giving grudgingly?

5. Prayer is the means by which God heightens the moral sensitivities of man. In prayer, God set boundaries for Adam—He gave warnings. When has a season of prayer left you with a clear leading you felt was intended to protect you?

6. Prayer is God in pursuit, God coming after man. In Genesis, it is God who pursues. Have you ever felt that God was pursuing you? Here, God refuses to let Adam hide. He refuses to let Adam's failure snuff out the relationship. The pursuing God acts in a redemptive manner. The relationship, though damaged, is salvaged. God refuses to let go of man! What grace!

7. Adam responds wrongly by shifting the blame (3:12). Have you discovered that the best approach, the most effective way to come to God, is in total honesty? God knows. He sees. In dishonesty, we don't hide from Him; we begin to hide our "selves" (vv. 7-11). We split ourselves in a way that renders us less than authentic. Wholeness demands integrity—especially with God in the privacy of prayer.

### Insights

Isn't it interesting that in the first two encounters between God and man, man is silent? God initiates. He does so even after man has sinned. When Adam and Eve violated the very boundaries about which they were warned, God still came to them. He repaired the relational breach with a sacrifice (Gen. 3:21). He covered man. He corrected, but He didn't spare them all the consequences (vv. 17-19).

Sin damaged man's strategic dominion. It injured the marriage relationship. Yet, God would not allow sin to completely sever the relationship. What grace! God wants communion with man more than man desires communion with Him. No other faith offers such a God!

# PRAYER GIVES PEACE

A king commissioned a contest among artists. Whoever could depict perfect peace on a canvas would win the King's admiration and a great treasure. Two entries were in the final review. One setting was so serene it seemed the epitome of peace and tranquillity. "Oohs" and "ahs" resounded from spectators as the painting was unveiled. Every detail was well ordered. Nothing was out of place. It was a picture of perfect peace. It was, everyone assumed, the sure contest winner.

The other entry was unveiled. It drew an immediate gasp. The canvas depicted everything but serenity. A massive waterfall dominated the scene. Angry, white foam and spray could almost be felt; the painting seemed so real. The deafening roar of the rumbling falls was implicit. The sky was dark, laden with streaks of lightning. The painting shouted: a stormy sky . . . thunder . . . lightning . . . rain . . . tumbling and roaring water. It seemed the very opposite of peace.

Then someone noticed that in the center of the painting, behind the waterfall in the cleft of the rock, a songbird had built a nest.

Sheltered by recessed rock, the songbird sat on her nest, confidently joining nature's symphony as if she had been assigned a melodious solo. You could almost hear her sing. Everyone knew this was the picture of perfect peace—to be in the cleft of the rock in the middle of a raging storm . . . *and sing!*

"In Me you may have peace," Jesus said, but "in the world you will have tribulation" (John 16:33). Peace is the effect on a heart quieted by the unmistakable sense of God's presence. It is unbroken communion with Him, and this is the essence of prayer. Much of our current anxiety can be traced to the lack of a daily, consistent, unhurried time with God. When even our devotional times are frantic, we can expect little peace in other areas of life.

# What Is Prayer?

John Bunyan declared:

> Prayer is the sincere, sensible, affectionate pouring out of the heart or soul to God, through Christ, in the strength and assistance of the Holy Spirit, for such things as God has promised, or according to the Word of God, for the good of the Church, with submission in faith to the will of God.[1]

Prayer demands sincerity, authenticity, a lack of hypocrisy. No duplicity is allowed. It must be rational, rooted in biblical truth and spiritual reality. It must involve the heart, the pouring out of the inner self. Passion is demanded. It was said that John Fletcher, author and pastor, stained the walls of his room by the breath of his prayer. He would pray all night, with earnestness.

Yet, prayer is neither a fervent effort of flesh or will, nor a self-control exercise based on Christian logic. Good praying demands divine partnership accomplished only by the strength and assistance of God, the Holy Spirit. It is bound to biblical promises and principles. It rises above the temporal, the earthly, and touches eternal Kingdom purposes. It is offered in faith, yet with submission to God's will. Henri Nouwen noted:

[Prayer is] no easy matter. It demands a relationship in which you allow the other to enter into the very center of your person, to speak there, to touch the sensitive core of your being, and allow the other to see so much that you would rather leave in darkness.[2]

I had been in ministry for more than twenty-five years when *I admitted to God* that I didn't understand prayer. Then the Prayer Summit movement allowed me to spend days at retreat centers with pastors of almost every denomination. We prayed morning, noon, and night. We encountered God. I was immeasurably enriched and forever changed. I had found the heart of ministry— the pursuit of His presence. Still, I longed to understand *the workings* of prayer.

My quest ultimately sent me back to Scripture—specifically, to *the prayers of the Bible*. Those prayers provided insights that radically changed my perspective. Prayer, I discovered, wasn't fundamentally "asking of God"; it was more than *petition*. Nor was the center of prayer passionate *intercession*. It wasn't simply "talking to God" or any one of a host of other valuable prayer functions: meditation, supplication, beseeching, crying out, petition, adoration, confession, thanksgiving, praise, and more. Prayer involves discerning, wrestling, resting, pulling down, rooting out, warfare, reconciliation, agreement, watching. It encompasses all of these, but it is more than the sum total of these components.

## DEFINING PRAYER

Prayer can be most simply understood in three categories: *communion, petition,* and *intercession*. All these are wrapped in a fourth—*thanksgiving*.

**Communion**—the heart of prayer is communion with God.

**Petition**—asking things of God, making requests—is possible only because of the communal relationship we have with the Father, through Jesus (John 14:13; 15:16; 16:23, 26).

**Intercession** is the position in the middle. It involves our duty as believers to pray for others, particularly for those who lack a vital saving relationship with Christ. But this is possible only because we ourselves are in such a redeemed relationship.

**Thanksgiving** is the overflow of a heart that recognizes what gifts God has given us through Christ. We tell Him we are grateful.

## Communion With God Is More Than Meditation

If the heart of prayer is *communion* with God, how do we enter into such communion? Quiet reflection is increasingly viewed as being synonymous with biblical prayer. But prayer is not simply reflectively and deductively thinking your way through some crisis or life decision, even if that process acknowledges God.

Eastern meditation is currently an American rage, but its focus is the subjective inner self. It calls for you to *empty* your mind. Christian meditation is different; it is objective and focused on Christ, His character, and His life in us (Ps. 1:1-3). It calls for you to *fill* your mind with Christ and with Scripture. Rather than search for strength and answers from within, biblical praying calls us out of ourselves. Wisdom to solve life's complex problems and the power to triumph over them are not called out through focused spiritual reflection in the *inner self.* Christian prayer accepts our weakness, inadequacy, and frailty. It reaches beyond the self to God. He is so large the ever-expanding universe is too small for Him.

Prayer and Scripture go hand in hand. We hear God through the conduit of Scripture. Memorization and meditation write Scripture on the inner walls of our hearts. They inform our prayer life. Thus we come to see things from heaven's perspective. Christian meditation uses the lens of Scripture. When hidden in our hearts (Ps. 119:11), it creates inner reference points that cause a confident recognition of His will and way and a sharpened sense of discernment (John 14:26). Christ-centered meditation is a powerful means of quieting the soul. It stills the heart and shuts out the noisy world. It positions us to clearly hear God. But meditation cannot take the place of *verbal* prayer. Jesus says, "When you pray, *say* . . ." (Luke 11:2). He intended for us to *speak*, to pray *aloud*.

## Communion With God Demands Speech

A man who believes that *thinking* he loves his spouse is the same as saying, "I love you! Forgive me," is greatly mistaken. Hosea told Israel, "Take words with you, and return to the Lord. Say to Him, 'Take away all iniquity; receive us graciously'" (Hos. 14:2). Prayer involves intentional, verbal speech. *Thinking it* is not the same as *praying it*. God created man with the capacity for speech. The biblical God is a *speaking* God. He could have willed the universe by thought. Instead, He spoke it into existence. The capacity for speech sets the human species apart. It is a divine-like quality.

"Death and life," the Scriptures say, "are in the power of the tongue" (Prov. 18:21). In prayer, we declare God's life over death-like situations. We call, prophetically, for victory in situations that appear hopeless. Prayer is a life-altering force. I am not suggesting that our speech—in the form of prayer or the prophetic—has original, creative energy. Words have power, but only God's speech is *omnipotent*.

Borrowing biblical language, our words are potent but not omnipotent. Powerful moments come when our voices join God's voice, echoing heaven's will on earth. We express into our time-space world what God is saying from His throne in heaven. Spirit-quickened prayers lend our human voices to His divine voice. Make no mistake—Bible-based, Spirit-led, prayerful speech is powerful. Wesley declared, "God governs by the prayers of His people." The alignment of heaven and earth by prayer sets off global changes.

## Communion With God Is Praying Beyond Words

Something happens when thoughts are spoken, even when we are alone in prayer. Some words have eternal impact. The experience of hearing ourselves say a certain thing has an effect that thought alone does not produce. Still, prayer is more than words; it is . . .

> . . . deeper than words. The total content of the prayers of Jesus can be repeated in less than fifteen minutes. Prayer is present in the soul before it has been formulated in words. And it abides in the soul after the last words of prayer have passed over our lips.[3]

You haven't prayed until you have prayed yourself to silence. Pour out your soul and you declare your love and allegiance to the Lord. You wrestle with the will of God. Then you submit, declaring you are at peace with the assertion of His will. In such moments, there are no more words to be said. Ole Hallesby wrote:

> There come times when I have nothing more to tell God. If I were to continue to pray in words, I would have to repeat what I have already said. At such times it is wonderful to say to God, "May I be in Thy presence, Lord? I have nothing more to say to Thee, but I do love to be in Thy presence."[4]

A sweet and searing silence laces your heart to the heart of God. You know that He loves you and He knows that you deeply love Him. You sense He has heard. An everything-is-going-to-be-all-right peace comes. Jonathan Edwards describes the effect of such prayer:

> My sense of divine things gradually increased, and became more and more lively, and had more . . . inward sweetness. The appearance of everything was altered; there seemed to be, as it were a calm, sweet cast, or appearance of divine glory, in almost everything.

> God's excellency, His wisdom, His purity and love seemed to appear in everything; in the sun, moon, and stars; in the clouds, and blue sky; in the grass, flowers, trees; in the water, and all nature . . . singing forth, with a low voice my contemplations of the Creator and Redeemer.[5]

Prayer demands words. You have to talk with God, describe passionately your situation, your perspective, your needs. Scriptural language enlarges your capacity to express your heart. You may pray in the Spirit, but in the end you discover that language alone cannot express your heart. Words are vessels that help empty the soul. Deeper levels of prayer are impossible without this emptying.

When you go beyond words, however, you come to the sweetest level of prayer. John Bunyan said, "In prayer, it is better to have heart without words, than words without heart." Unity with God is the heart of prayer. Prayer produces its ultimate state when the Spirit seamlessly reveals Christ to us and through us. He prays for us. He speaks through us. We give voice to the Spirit, praying as God would have us pray, until as yielded vessels even the tongue, the unruly member, is in perfect submission. There is congruence, inner harmony. An all-is-well, God-is-on-His-throne disposition governs. We are centered in God's love. Brother Lawrence says the essence of prayer is this sense of *His presence*.[6]

## WHY PRAY?

Sidlow Baxter declared, "No blessing of the Christian life becomes continually possessed unless we are men and women of regular, daily, unhurried secret lingerings in prayer."[7] For some "prayer is a form of spiritual gambling: you make your needs and desires known and hope for the best."[8] Others ask, "Why should we pray? God knows what we need before we ask" (Matt. 6:8). Some believe that God, out of goodness alone, will automatically take care of their needs. He cares for the birds of the air and lilies of the field; will He not automatically take care of us? The answer is a surprising "No!"

"You do not have," James said, "because you do not ask" (4:2). Prayer is the process by which the believer appropriates heaven's resources out of the abundance of Christ. God could act apart from prayer, but He chooses to act with prayer. The place to start with all our needs is prayer. James was asking needy believers, "Why don't you pray?" Some Christians there had prayed, but God didn't answer (v. 3). Their motives were wrong. They were praying for selfish reasons. God refuses to answer prayers that deepen our bondage to self. His goal is to liberate and transform us.

## God Loves Company

The Christians to whom James was writing had come to see prayer only as a means of acquisition. God is more than the clerk of heaven's storehouse. He wants a relationship with us. The Greek gods were a self-centered lot. World religions are full of gods that appear indifferent or so transcendent they are unknowable. In Christianity, God is a friend to man. He walks and talks with us. He is moved with the feeling of our infirmities. Search the faiths of the world and you will find no other God like this One!

God wants company. He created man with a capacity for fellowship. After Creation, He came walking through the garden looking for Adam. From Genesis to Jesus, we have a friendly, talking God. Prayer is the means by which He fellowships with us. Prayer is relational, and relationships necessitate communication. But deep relationships extend beyond language to a wordless connection possible only after all that needs to be said has been said. In prayer, we find the acceptance and affirmation of God. God relates to us, loves us, likes us, encourages and nurtures us. He directs and warns us, convicts and corrects us, grows and develops us. All of this happens in the context of prayer.

## Prayer Is a Privilege

The very privilege of Christian prayer is such a precious gift that we hardly understand how extraordinary it is. We take it for granted! We assume that all people pray and understand it in similar ways. A Muslim must pray in Arabic, but he is never sure that Allah hears. A Hindu must seek the services of a Brahman to do his praying for him. Buddhism teaches that we are to embrace suffering, to not expect an answer. The Buddhist must save himself.

Who do we think we are to ask *God* to serve *us*? To grant us a hearing, then rally heaven and respond? Christian prayer is astoundingly different from other religions. We are so blessed! We may not only approach the throne of the King of the universe, but we are told to do so with boldness. Such an act is unthinkably laden with grace. Christian prayer—what a privilege!

In the Old Testament, Israel knew God as a Father, but no one called Him "*my* Father!" The New Testament perspective is wonderfully different. We stand on the Resurrection side of time. Christ died and rose from the dead, rescuing Old Testament saints from death's prison. He is on the throne in heaven. He has sent the Holy Spirit to live in our hearts. He has given us the privilege of prayer in His name. We call God "Father," through our relationship with Christ! Sealed by the Spirit, we are afforded the opportunity to live in unbroken fellowship with God.

## Heaven's Way of Blessing

Prayer is heaven's way of blessing. Andrew Murray said:

> God's intense longing to bless seems in some sense to be graciously limited by His dependence on intercession. God regards intercession as the highest expression of His people's readiness to receive and to yield themselves wholly to the working of His almighty power.[9]

*God's intense longing to bless*—what a concept! According to Murray, God *intensely longs* to bless, but that "longing to bless" is limited! How could any intense longing of the Sovereign God be limited? *Graciously . . . by His dependence upon our intercession*— God could act apart from prayer, but He chooses not to. Prayer invites God's involvement in our world. Prayer changes us. It readies us to more fully partner with God. Our prayerlessness breaks the heart of God. Remedies for all of our problems are a prayer away. Our lack of prayer keeps us in need. It frustrates our participation in the will of God. What blessings we miss by our prayerlessness.

## Prayer Taps the Bounty in the Estate of Christ

Imagine your parents having a house full of family treasures you desire. To take them while they are alive would be unthinkable. If they have a will, you could not, even at the tragic news of their death, race to their house and claim the best treasures. A will is a legal document, supported by the court system and its police power. The authority of the state stands behind the enforcement of a legal will. One can control the distribution of what he or she acquired—even after he is gone—through a will. You are an heir. You have an inheritance traceable to Christ—a wealth of treasures. The writer of Hebrews reminds us that a will and testament is valid only when the maker of the will dies (9:16-17). When Christ died, He left an expressed will. The New Testament is His last will.

## Our Basis of Appeal Rests on Covenant Promises

The only way you and I have a claim on the court of heaven is through our covenant relationship with Jesus (Heb. 9:18-20; 12:23-24). Grace answered the Law and satisfied its demands (Eph. 2:1-9). So it is our covenant that gives us the privilege of prayer, of accessing the throne of God (Rom. 5:1-2). We can file a petition, a claim on the storehouses of heaven, based on the finished work of Christ. By prayer, we enter heaven's courtroom and draw from the riches of the estate of Christ (Eph. 3:8; Phil. 4:19). The Holy Spirit is our counselor and the executor of Christ's estate. Jesus said, "All things that the Father has are Mine" (John 16:15). He said the Holy Spirit "will take of what is Mine" and give it to us (see vv. 13-15). The Father himself decrees the allocations (see v. 23).

Paul tells us that it is the Holy Spirit who distributes gifts to believers (1 Cor. 12:7, 11). These are "gracious bestowments." Out of grace, He divides them "individually as He wills." We are heirs, joint heirs with Christ (Rom. 8:17; Titus 3:7; Heb. 6:17; James 2:5). Praying and wishing are not the same. We pray, based on the promises of God in Christ. We have no other basis on which we might ask God for anything. Prayer demands an open Bible. Many Christians are wishing not praying based on Scripture.

## Prayer Invites the Kingdom of God

Jesus taught what we commonly call "the Lord's Prayer." In truth, it is the disciples' prayer. In Matthew 6:9, it is a model, a template for prayer ("In this manner . . . pray"). In Luke 11:2, it is a prayer to be prayed repeatedly ("When you pray . . ."). It is both a form to be repeated as the prayer of our heart and a model of the way we should pray. Never once in this prayer do you find *me*, *my*, or *I*. Instead you find *our*, *us* and *we*. Prayer cannot be only about our narrow slice of pain. It pulls us out of our little world. In prayer, we request that His exiled kingdom break into our time-space world. We express dissidence in the face of the rising darkness. We declare allegiance to His rejected kingship. We plead for His will to be done and His rule asserted. This prayer begins and ends with Kingdom. This is the overall purpose of all prayer—to bring the earth, beginning with us, under His lordship.

As agents of this Kingdom, we are to be different from the world around us. We are dependent on His hand for daily bread. We are a forgiving people because we have been forgiven. We are a holy people who do not want to be led into temptation or overpowered with evil desire.

The heart of Christianity is faith for the day, love for others, and purity in life. Superstitious repetition is a pagan notion Jesus warned against (Matt. 6:7). Prayer should borrow form from Scripture, but ultimately, it has to rise from the heart. The Jewish rabbis taught "Index Prayers." These were abbreviated outlines for prayer. They were single phrases to be memorized as a track for prayer. Each phrase suggested an item for more extensive and spontaneous prayer.

The prayer that Jesus taught appears to be an "Index Prayer!" We pray it . . . and expand it. Drawing from the language of Scripture, we enlarge our capacity for expression, always making the prayer our own. Remember, however, form will never take the place of fire. Mere language or prayer phrases cannot take the place of deep yearning.

# HINDRANCES TO PRAYER

R. A. Torrey lists seven hindrances to prayer:

1. *Selfishness*. The prayer may be for things otherwise appropriate, but the motive may be wrong. Praying with self at the center is praying amiss (James 4:3).

2. *Sin*. "Your iniquities have separated you from your God; and your sins have hidden His face from you, so that He will not hear" (Isa. 59:2). Sin hinders prayer. Tears do not aid such prayers (Mal. 2:13). Only repentance can clear the way for a legitimate hearing in heaven's courtroom (Joel 2:12; Acts 8:22).

3. *Idolatry.* Anything that occupies the place in the heart designed for God is an idol. It need not be physical or tangible. Idolatry is a spiritual matter; the image is its symbol (Ezek. 14:3).

4. *Stinginess.* A giving God hears a giving people. "Whoever shuts his ears to the cry of the poor will also cry himself and not be heard" (Prov. 21:13). The giving God wants a giving people. The more liberal we are, the more liberal He is (Luke 6:38).

5. *Unforgiveness.* "Whenever you stand praying . . . forgive" (Mark 11:25). Prayer demands forgiveness. If we who are imperfect and prone to mistakes want mercy and acceptance before a perfect and holy God, we must be more gracious toward those whose flaws affect us. We must forgive, if we want forgiveness.

6. *Sensitivity in the Family.* Husbands are called to give honor to their wives because they are "heirs together of the grace of life" (1 Peter 3:7). A lack of sensitivity between the husband and the wife will "hinder" prayers.

7. *Unbelief.* When you pray, you must believe. "Ask in faith, with no doubting" (James 1:6). A lack of faith in prayer is likened to a ship without an anchor in a turbulent sea—back and forth, up and down. Double dimensional instability! Faith, that intangible, anchors prayer. It grounds it. With invisible hands, it lays hold on heaven's promises and wrestles them to the earth. Prayer that lacks faith doesn't "receive anything from the Lord" (v. 7).[10]

## Questions for Discussion

1. Which of Torrey's seven hindrances would be your greatest hindrance to prayer?

2. Can you give a definition for *prayer*?

3. List three categories of prayer. Does this help you gain a more balanced perspective of prayer?

4. How is Christian meditation different from non-Christian meditation?

5. Do you agree that prayer demands words? Why?

6. How is Christian prayer different from prayer in other world religions?

7. Do you ever pray with an open Bible? Are you wishing or praying? Do you see the relationship between prayer and the estate of Christ?

# Chapter 2

# Personal Prayer

**Foundation Study:** Man's Pursuit of God

**Bible Focus:** Hebrews 11:6

### Central Truth

The goal of prayer is intimacy with God himself, not the acquisition of things.

## Key Principles

Extraordinary outcomes to prayer results in common men of faith being thrust into positions of power and influence. Propelled by encounters with God, they impact nations. History pivots. Such outcomes are rarely on the radar screen of these great men; they happened as they pursued God and obeyed Him. Too much discussion about faith is framed in terms of what we can get, but the great acquisition in prayer is God himself. The greatest change that comes to us is the transformation from trying to convince Him to please us, to a growing desire in us to please Him (John 8:29; 2 Cor. 5:9; Col. 1:9-10). The rewards of praying are greater than the answers to prayer.

## Points of Emphasis

1. According to Hebrews 11:6, God "is a *rewarder* of those who diligently seek" . . . answers? breakthrough? revival?

No. He rewards those who diligently seek . . . *Him*! God himself is the great reward of prayer.

2. Lay hold of *the One who answers* instead of merely laying hold of *an answer*! Seeking answers and not the One who answers is like leaving the well with a cup of water, when we could have had the well itself. Jacob was changed as he wrestled—not with the promise, but with the One who promised.

3. "Without faith it is impossible to please Him" (v. 6). Do you attempt to get God to please you in prayer, or do you ask to do what pleases Him? A benchmark for healthy prayer is, "Father, I want to please You!" Are you a God-pleaser? Or a man-pleaser?

4. "He who comes to God"—that's a prayer term—"must believe that He is"! Prayer is not merely self-talk. God hears (John 11:41-42). Prayer impacts real things. The person who comes to God must also believe that He is "a rewarder," that He is a good God. How does your perception of God affect your prayer life?

5. The attack of the Evil One against faith is usually not against the existence or even the ability of God. It is against the *character* of God. Satan will whisper, "God can, but He *won't!*" In Genesis 3, he can be heard asking, "Did God say that?"—as if to imply, "You don't really believe Him, do you?" Such intrusions of doubt say, "You can't trust God!"

6. Perhaps the most important question is the question of God's love. In Romans 8:33-39, a parade of resistance lines up to "separate us from the love of God." Jude urges us to build ourselves up by prayer, keeping ourselves in the love of God (vv. 20-21). Paul asserts, "We are more than conquerors through Him who loved us" (Rom. 8:37). Nothing derails prayer or wounds faith like doubts about God's love.

7. Sometimes we use answers to prayer as a means of measuring God's love. If answers come, we feel loved; if they don't, we doubt. We may pray, "God, if You love me, do this or that." An arrangement that puts God in the position of having "to prove" His love is manipulation. Love precedes prayer. Faith soars when you know God loves you. If I really

believe God loves me, I have few doubts about His provision. My Father will hear and answer.

8. We sometimes get discouraged when answers don't come to prayer. God does answer prayer. Of 650 definitive prayers in the Bible, there are 450 recorded answers.[1] But prayer is more than a divine requisitioning system. God rewards us for seeking Him. And rewards are not the same as answers. The rewards of pursuing Him are greater than the answers.

## Insights

In Matthew 6, Jesus promised a "reward" for praying. "When you pray," He said, assuming we would pray, "go into your room" (v. 6). He expected us to maintain a secret place for prayer. There God would meet us. When we go to our secret place for prayer, God races ahead of us. Sometimes He doesn't even disclose His presence. Jesus notes that "your Father who sees in secret will reward you openly" (Matt. 6:6). God hides in my closet and then manifests with me in the public square. The private moments of surrender translate into public God-moments punctuated with His presence.

# PRAYER, THE DEFINING MARK OF A CHRISTIAN

Prayer is the defining mark of a true Christian. *He is no Christian who does not pray.* Martin Luther said, "As a shoemaker makes a shoe, and a tailor makes a coat, so ought a Christian to pray."[2] Herbert Lockyer said, "Man has been described as a 'praying animal'. . . . [Prayer is] "the deepest instinct of the soul of man."[3] It is impossible to find in history a truly great man of God who was not a great man of prayer. Bishop Asbury, renowned in Methodist circles, would rise at 4 a.m. and pray for two hours. It is said that Martin Luther regularly spent the first two hours of the day in prayer. Adoniram Judson's work in China was aided by his midnight prayer experiences.

Henry Martyn, the English missionary, said there evolved a "strangeness" in his soul when he had spent too much time in public administration and too little time in private communion with God. William Wilberforce called that "living far too public" and starving the soul.[4] Robert Murray McCheyne vowed to not see *people* before he had met with God. In many churches, prayer time brings a seemingly endless recital of needs, usually without any thanksgiving reports. This weekly episode becomes a silent faith crusher. Nothing is so small that it should not be taken to God in prayer, but petition is not the whole of prayer. Petition without a clear gaze at answered prayer is unhinged praying. Prayer is not primarily a means of acquisition from God.

The heart of prayer is *communion*—oneness with God, unity, the celebration of our union and peace with God through Jesus Christ. We can ask things only because we "abide in Him" (see John 14:3; 15:4-7). Without this vital relationship, there is no basis on which we can make requests. This connection allows us to intercede for others, especially those who have no relationship with Christ. Yet, it is simple communion that we most often fail to nurture in our prayer times.

Living in constant communion with God is the heart of prayer and the essence of our faith. Everything rises and falls on the grace that flows from a healthy, personal prayer life. Our time with God demonstrates our love, our longing for His presence, and our willingness to be obedient. Through prayer, we present ourselves on God's altar.

Fifteen times the prayer life of Jesus is noted in the Gospels— three in Matthew and four in Mark, Luke, and John. "The Man Christ Jesus prayed; prayed much; needed to pray; loved to pray."[5] He began His ministry in prayer and ended it in prayer. He prayed in the morning (Mark 1:35). He spent days in prayer

(Luke 4:42; 5:15-16; 9:18-31; Mark 6:30-31). He prayed at His baptism (Luke 3:21-22). He prayed on the Mount of Transfiguration (Luke 9:29). When He returned to the Father, it was to pray (John 14:16; 16:26; Heb. 7:25). At the same time, He sent His disciples to a prayer meeting (Luke 24:49).

His life was a life of prayer. Jesus came to the earth to pray. To be like Jesus means to pray.

# MARKS OF AN EFFECTIVE PRAYER LIFE

## Prayer and the Secret Place

A secret life of prayer is the key to successful public ministry. Jesus said, "When you pray, go into your room . . . shut your door, pray" (Matt. 6:6). Jonathan Edwards believed this fact:

> If you live in the neglect of secret prayer, you show your good will to neglect all the worship of God. He that prays only when he prays with others would not pray at all were it not that the eyes of others are on him. He that will not pray where no one but God sees does not pray at all out of respect to God or with regard to his all-seeing eye.[6]

The practice of personal, at-home, daily prayer has reached an abysmal low. Prayer at church can't replace prayer at home. When Christians do pray during the week, they pray on the run. No quality relationship can be sustained with such a low investment of time and priority. Jesus assumed we would have a "secret place of prayer!" Luke describes Jesus praying "in a certain place" (Luke 11:1), indicating a favorite spot for prayer. Intimacy with God requires a "secret place of prayer"! It may be a closet or a corner, a room or a rocking chair. It may be a garden or a vista point. Such a place is sacred. Being in the place is a signal to God of our seeking, searching heart.

## Prayer, the Secret to Spiritual Power

An encouraging trend is emerging. Serious Christians are creating prayer rooms in their homes. Rooms range in size from a large closet to a spare bedroom. Size is not nearly as important as the significance of the room. It should be a safe place to meet God and pour out one's heart. Out of private meetings with God come public encounters with Him.

Edwin Tull is fondly remembered as "the chaplain at Lee University." He was raised in a non-Pentecostal home on the Eastern shore of Maryland. When his mother was bed-ridden with a crippling arthritic condition, the local physician informed the family there was nothing else he could do. The family felt hopeless, and helpless. Someone said, "There is a preacher at the Church of God who believes God can heal." They called him. He came.

The hands of Mrs. Tull were drawn and disfigured. She was immobilized. The praying preacher was not intimidated by the sight of her crippled condition. He prayed. God came. Those present watched deformed hands straighten. They saw a bed-fast woman rise and dance before the Lord. That's when Edwin Tull fell to the floor. That moment changed his life forever. He met the God of the New Testament, and his whole family was swept into Pentecost. What is the secret to the pastor's power? God shows up in public with those who meet Him privately. The secret place of prayer for Pastor C. J. (Pop) Abbott was by his bedside. So frequently did he kneel there, so fervently did he pray there, that two grooves had been worn into the floor by the knees of the praying pastor.

## Prayer, Moving From Duty to Delight

At the Tabernacle, days began and ended at the altar. The life of Jesus was marked by prayer, sometimes at night. His habit was to rise early to pray (Mark 1:35). David said, "Early will I seek You" (Ps. 63:1). Clyde Cranford quoted a truism: "Every morning, lean your arms on the window sill of heaven and gaze into the face of thy Lord."[7] Charles Spurgeon said, "Prayer should be the key of the day and the lock of the night."[8]

Most of us think of prayer as *works*! Prayer is seen as a duty, not as a glorious privilege. Some approach prayer as necessary but undesirable: "I know I *should* pray. To grow in Christ I *have* to pray!" "If we are going to see revival, we *must* pray!" It is as if prayer is a kind of *spiritual castor oil*—not pleasant, but essential. We *should* pray, this is true.

Further, we *must* pray, but healthy prayer moves beyond *duty* to *delight*. When we are drawn to God by love, not necessity, we long for His presence. Imagine saying to God: "In order to get this noble outcome, how much time do I *have to* spend with You? An hour? What would fifteen minutes get? I want this blessing, this revival, but I want it with as little time spent alone with You as possible!"

Such speech would be reprehensible, shocking, appalling. But do we sometimes exhibit this behavior? If we only want the *effect* of prayer and not a deeper relationship with God himself, we reveal our true hearts. Nine of ten Americans (78 percent) pray every week. Half pray several times a day. The average prayer time is about five minutes.[9] These are fleeting prayers, prayed on the run between business appointments.

Delight, however, makes prayer itself the main agenda. All other business is set aside. The day is spent with God! Daily prayer is an anchor. It is a thermostat that regulates our temperament. By prayer, we tune our hearts to the music of heaven and ready ourselves to serve. We hear His voice and are empowered to respond.

Few Christians have riveting spiritual encounters in prayer every day. As we faithfully set ourselves aside unto Him, God hides under our noses. But our daily private discipline is inevitably linked to unpredictable and delightful encounters with God in the public square.

Contrasting our reticence, Luther said, "The devil . . . is not lazy or careless, and our flesh is too ready and eager to sin. It is disinclined to the spirit of prayer." The great Reformer urged:

> Let prayer be the first business of the morning and the last at night. Guard yourself carefully against those false, deluding ideas which tell you, 'Wait a little while. I will pray in an hour; first I must attend to this or that.' Such thoughts get you away from prayer into other affairs which so hold your attention and involve you that nothing comes of prayer for that day"[10]

In the book *The Spirit of Discipline*, Francis Paget describes "the tremendous power of habit; the constant, silent growth with which it creeps and twines about the soul, until its branches clutch and grip like iron." He warns that "the habitual drift, the natural tendency of our unclaimed thought, should be towards high and pure and gladdening things."

Discipline makes the difference: "the leisure time of life may either be a man's garden or his prison."[11] The heart cry of every Christian should be for a daily rendezvous with Jesus. Adoniram Judson, the great missionary to Burma, prayed "seven times a day." Still, he labored six years without a convert. Thirty-eight years later, however, he had recorded 210,000 conversions. One in every fifty-eight Burmese were believers. Fruitfulness follows faithfulness. Luther said, "If I should neglect prayer but a single day, I should lose a great deal of the fire of faith."[12]

## Prayer, Worshipful Love

We reduce prayer to a mere component in a worship service. Prayer in its purest form is worship; but the heart of worship is our love of God. C. S. Lewis believed that "in the process of being worshiped, God communicates His presence to man."[13] The incomparable Christ is the treasure in the field, the pearl of great price, worth more than the whole world (Matt. 13:44-46). This discovery shifts our values, and reorients and realigns our lives.

Love demands passion. The Song of Solomon says, "Let him kiss me . . . [his] love is better than wine" (1:2). Here, two lovers are on fire with desire for each other. The church at Ephesus was still standing, still working, still enduring, still upholding truth; but they had left their passion (Rev. 2:4). This rebuke called for repentance. It predicted total backsliding.

Passion is essential in our relationship with God. William Cowper says he had "known such exaltation that he thought he would die from excess of joy."[14] In the Song of Solomon, love is intoxicating, and a simple kiss is disorienting, entrancing. Our culture is passionate about everything but the right thing. People tend to gravitate to sports, recreation, hobbies, money, automobiles, the adult toys we have come to afford, affluent lifestyles, and more. Passion belongs in two places: in our relationship with God and in our love for our spouse (Eph. 5:25).

## Prayer and the Exiled Bridegroom

We misplace passion. We think loving the Church is the same as loving God, but it isn't. The Church is the bride of Christ, His vehicle for service and witness. It is the visible expression of Christ in the earth. We serve the Church, but our passion belongs to Jesus. The Church is not about itself, it is about Jesus. It is rightly constituted by members passionately in love with Christ, looking and living as if He might return today. *Worshipful devotion* to the Bridegroom can never be satisfied by *dutiful work*. Working for Him is not the same as worshiping Him. Worship at church cannot stand in the place of a daily, personal, at-home relationship with God. This does not diminish service to the church, it intensifies it. Because of this love, I work, witness, and live in the blessed hope of His return. My work for Christ flows out of my worship. Spurgeon said, "He who lives without prayer, he who lives with little prayer, he who seldom reads the Word, and he who seldom looks up to heaven for a fresh influence from on high—he will be the man whose heart will become dry and barren."[15]

## Prayer, the Empowerment to Action

You hear the expression, "There! I have said it!" Sometimes a good feeling follows; sometimes it is regret. Saying it empowers an idea in a way that mere thinking never does. Saying a thing gives birth to possibility. It pushes an inner thought to the outside. Others hear it, touch it, examine it, and agree or disagree. It unifies. It polarizes. Actions follow words; we talk ourselves into doing things. What we allow ourselves to *say* rises out of thoughts we express. Things happens when we express deep needs and longings, hopes and dreams, hurts and fears. Saying it is different from thinking it. "I am willing to go anywhere! Use me, God!" Or, "God, I don't want to do this!" Or, "God, I can't forgive him. I can't love her!" Such honest prayers reveal an inner resistance, but persistent praying changes a person. "O God, help me love him. Help me forgive her. O God, I want to please You!"

The Bible is a record of prayer—of praying men and women and what they accomplished. Praying believers have been change-agents whose mark on history seems timeless. Moved to act in faith, they accomplished things far beyond their own limited capabilities. The Scripture is a record of culture shifts effected by energy from another world. Prayer moves us to action.

## Prayer, a Means of Filtering Toxic Thoughts

Prayer is a soul filter. Luther said the storms of life provide the opportunity for us to empty our cargo, "to speak with earnestness, to open the heart and pour out what lies at the bottom."[16] Alone with God in prayer, I am safe in pouring out my deepest feelings. Here, a therapy takes place. A cleansing comes. The Psalms give us blunt prayer language, full of despair and sometimes loaded with less-than-noble motives. But in the end, the psalmist turns upward and is reoriented. "But, I will wait for You!" (see Ps. 59:1-10; also 71:14; 75:9; 77:10; 119:69, 78).

In prayer, we pray through our objections. We overcome our noncompliance. We confront our doubts. We face our fears. We *pray through* such things, and God gives us grace. In the garden, Jesus said, "My heart is nearly breaking." The Greek word is *ekthambeo*. It means to be thrown into a state of fear or thoroughly amazed, to be astounded or struck with terror.[17] We can hardly imagine Jesus like this. "Father, if it is possible, let this cup pass" (Matt. 26:39). He does not discuss this openly with the disciples. He is with them, yet removed. Only the Father can help Him with this need. In prayer, Jesus moved to the place of total surrender. He prayed Himself into complete alignment with the Father's will. He silences any resistance in His flesh. Prayer summons the strength of heaven for the task (Luke 22:43). An angel strengthened Him. This is prayer.

## Pray With an Open Bible

We allow an unhealthy practice when we consistently pray without a Bible. Good prayer is over an open Bible. Loran Livingston often tells his growing congregation, "Read the Word, and pray!" The Bible is the Christian's prayer book. It is not to be read passively, it is to be read as if one were having a conversation with God. It is a love letter as well as an instruction manual for life. You read, and you respond in prayer. You borrow from the concepts and language of the Bible. You wrestle. You ask God, "What does this mean . . . to me . . .

right now?" In the pages of Scripture, we find the clearest and soundest resonance of God's voice. Walter Wangerin describes praying Scripture in this way:

> Imagine . . . the Psalm is like a house already built and that you are invited to enter there to make it your own. Praying from within the Psalm is to pray your own prayer . . . though you use words already written, you have become the present and living soul within those words.[18]

The Bible is to be prayed! You must enter the Scripture and pray from within it. Luther said when he was cool or joyless, the condition was always traced to a deficit in prayer. Aware of the capacity of the "flesh and the devil" to "impede and obstruct" prayer, he developed a habitual response to coolness of heart.

> I take my little Psalter, hurry to my room, or . . . to where a congregation is assembled and, as time permits, I say quietly to myself and word-for-word the Ten Commandments, the Creed, and, if I have time, some words of Christ or Paul, or some Psalm, just as a child might do.[19]

"Prayer itself," Fosdick reminds us, "is a great conqueror of perverse moods."[20] Spurgeon wrote, "We should pray when we are in a praying mood, for it would be sinful to neglect so fair an opportunity. We should pray when we are not in a praying mood because it would be dangerous to remain in so unhealthy a condition."[21]

## Prayer, a Means of Purification

The old saying goes, "What's down in the well comes up in the bucket!" Nothing will promote personal holiness as much as prayer and the study of the Word. The great Scottish pastor and writer Robert Murray McCheyne was asked what he felt was the greatest need of his congregation. "The holiness of their pastor," he responded.[22]

The church today is minimizing sin. We redefine it as merely a "mistake." To be sure, any sin is a mistake, but it is more than stubbing the toe. Sin is deadly. It is toxic to relationships. It is a poison to the soul. Christians should never act as if the free blood of Jesus can casually be splashed about to cover just any sin. Such blood isn't cheap, even if grace is free. Nathan said to David, "The Lord . . . has put away your sin; you shall not die" (2 Sam. 12:13). Wow! *David could have died.* "The wages of sin is death" (Rom. 6:23). Grace was never intended to foster the careless attitude toward sin that has emerged in the contemporary church. Such a view not only misunderstands grace, it is a delusion (vv. 1-2). Sin kills. It is to be avoided at all costs. Grace is designed to not only deliver us *from* the curse of the law, but to deliver us to another law—the life-giving law of righteousness (v. 18).

John Bunyan said, "Prayer will make a man cease from sin, or sin will entice a man to cease from prayer. Pray often, for prayer is a shield to the soul, a sacrifice to God, and a scourge for Satan."[23] Over an open Bible in prayer, I find myself in need of change. Before the mirror of the Word, I see myself as falling short. Bunyan cried out, "Oh, the startling holes that the heart hath in the time of prayer!" Repentance is the healthy reaction of an upright heart. Before God, we "confess our sins" and "He is faithful and just to forgive us our sins and to cleanse us from all unrighteousness" (1 John 1:9). Before one another we confess our "trespasses," and He heals us (James 5:16). "We are never closer to God than in repentance. In humility and shame, we partake of the matchless grace of God, and the result is a deeper intimacy with Him and a greater sensitivity to His desires."[24]

William Carey notes, "Prayer—secret, fervent, believing prayer—lies at the root of all personal godliness."[25] The capacity to engage a holy God and not change demonstrates the insidious nature and strength of sin's hold within a person. Face-to-face with a holy God, the prophet cried out, "I am undone! . . . a man of unclean lips" (Isa. 6:5). So must we. Crooked hearts dodge repentance and remain deluded; tender hearts break before God. Richard Foster notes:

> To pray is to change. Prayer is the central avenue God uses to transform us. If we are unwilling to change, we will abandon prayer as a noticeable characteristic of our lives. The closer we come to the heartbeat of God, the more we see our need and the more we desire to be conformed to Christ.[26]

Prayer deals with toxins in the soul. It purifies. In prayer, I take my anger and cynicism, my unbelief and despair, my disappointment and fear of failure to God. There, in the presence of a holy and loving Father, I find myself saying, "But God, I really want to be like You. I want to be free of this. I want You to change me, strengthen my faith and cause me to triumph." If we would go to God in prayer with our deadly and carnal inclinations and not to our neighbor, if we would talk to no one about our hurts and disappointments until we talk to God, it would cure a great deal of gossip and slander in the church. Prayer corrects wrong thinking. It realigns character. It nudges us toward Christlikeness. Richard Foster adds, "When we pray, God slowly and graciously reveals to us our evasive actions and sets us free from them."[27]

## Living in an Atmosphere of Prayer

We are to "pray without ceasing" (1 Thess. 5:16). If prayer is verbal, *how* can we do it? If it involves religious activities, how is *this* possible? Prayer, at its deepest and purest level, is living in unbroken fellowship with God. Out of this communion, we offer our needs to God, and He enters into our lives with His bountiful supply. From this connection, we intercede for others.

In a state of peace, we engage in the warfare of prayer, confident of our victory. As Oswald Chambers observes, "Prayer is not an exercise. It is the life of the saint." Relationships need unhurried time. Our relationship with God is no exception. God's design was that once a week, an entire day was to be set aside to walk and talk with Him. The rhythm of our lives should make time for God. The feast days, Israel's holidays, were holy days, days to be spent advancing their relationship with Yahweh. God was on the calendar of His people, Israel—daily, weekly, monthly (the new moon), and seasonally (festivals and holy days). Is He on your calendar? R. A. Torrey said:

> When the devil sees a man or woman who really believes in prayer, who knows how to pray, and who really does pray, and, above all, when he sees a whole church on its face before God in prayer, "he trembles" as much as he ever did, for he knows that his day in that church or community is at an end.[28]

## Prayer Is Transformational

In our world, faith is increasingly marginalized. "Newton banished God from nature, Darwin banished Him from life, and Freud banished Him from His last stronghold, the soul."[29] Christ is seen as an additive to enrich our lives. Biblical principles are viewed as informative for a more productive life. Man supposedly has a small tear in his soul and the cross is a repair kit. Such notions are radically inferior to true New Testament perspective.

Christianity is not a sweet supplement. Christ did not come to make men *better*, He came to make men *new*. Theologian Emil Brunner said, "Only he who understands that sin is inexplicable, knows what it is!"[30] This is "the mystery of lawlessness" (2 Thess. 2:7). Human acts are sometimes bizarre and unthinkably wicked. Yet our culture rationalizes away a personal devil that tempts and twists the nature of men. We are getting help with evil (Eph. 2:2), so we must get help to do good.

Salvation is a liberation event, wresting us from the powers of darkness. It is the transfer from the body of Adam to the body of Christ (Rom. 5:12-21; 1 Cor. 15:45-49; Jude 23). It makes all things new. Saved and liberated, man is free to worship, to do right, to serve God. But this freedom must be exercised. Too many Christians define themselves in terms of what they don't do or where they no longer go. A man or woman is not free if he or she is only "free from." We must be "free to" pray and praise, to worship and witness, and to bless others and demonstrate love.

Freedom *from* is neutrality. It is the exercise of our new liberty in the disciplines of faith that move us forward and keep us free (Rom. 6:13, 16, 18-22). The discipline of prayer is at the heart of this new liberty. In a lifestyle of dependence, I am led, directed, and renewed by the Spirit. In humble dependence, my confidence in God grows. I hear His voice. I obey. I am being transformed. G. Campbell Morgan said, "The prayer life consists of life that is always upward and onward and Godward."[31]

# THE PROCESS OF PRAYER

Prayer is simple, even childlike. Yet, there is an order about prayer.

## Pray Always

Pray "on all occasions!" Prayer should be sprinkled into every aspect of our lives. It should be natural and spontaneous. By prayer, we invite God into our lives. So pray as you drive to work, as you sit in your home, as you look at the beauty of nature, and hear the birds sing. Pray when you entertain friends, and as your children come and go. Prayer must never be foreign to daily life.

Prayer is not to be a strange exercise offered once a week in a building with colored windows. We are to pray everywhere, about everything, and in doing so, we involve God in our lives. There is never a time when prayer is inappropriate. There is never a mood in which prayer is not fitting:

Pray when you are depressed (Ps. 42).

Pray when you are happy (9:2).

Pray when you are angry (4:4).

Pray when you are tempted (Matt. 4:1-11).

Pray when you are weak and feeling alone (Luke 22).

Pray when your faith seems to be failing you.

Be real with God (Matt. 26:41).

## Pray According to the Word

The Bible is our prayer book. From it we draw the language to pray. On the basis of its promises we argue our claims in the courtroom of heaven. By it we are guided to make corrections in our lives, change our plea, deepen our intensity, or discover some answer we had not seen before. From the pages of God's sacred Word, He speaks most clearly. Scripture comes alive. New meanings emerge. Our hearts are strangely warmed. Our minds understand. Our spirit is renewed. Pray with an open Bible. Make your prayers consistent with Scripture.

## Pray With the Enabling of the Holy Spirit

The Holy Spirit acts as a counselor in prayer. He aids our praying (Matt. 20:22; John 4:10; Rom. 8:26-27; Jude 20). So you may pray "in the Spirit," but you should always pray "with the Spirit." Prayer in the Spirit moves us from misguided to Spirit-directed praying. It prevents our "praying amiss" (James 4:3). "The Spirit . . . helps in our weaknesses. For we do not know what we should pray for . . . but the Spirit

Himself makes intercession . . . according to the will of God" (Rom. 8:26-27).

Praying by the Spirit moves us from uncertainty to a certain knowing. This is not something the head knows, but something about which the heart is certain. God has heard. He has answered. The matter is settled. But prayer needs balance.

We pray by the unction of the Spirit, but also "with understanding" (see 1 Cor. 14:15). We speak and pray mysteries, but prayer should also enlighten us. The mind is to be edified as well as the spirit. Prayer informs. It reveals. It uncovers hidden things and places them before us as logical and explicable concepts. Better praying isn't found by "trying harder" but by "yielding sooner." The quickening Spirit brings passion, but He also knows how to help us pray.

## Pray in the Name of Jesus (John 14:13; 15:16)

A majority of Americans believe that "all people pray to the same god . . . no matter what name they use for that spiritual being."[32] The name of Jesus is not a magic word Christians say at the end of a prayer. Its power is far beyond that. With the enthronement of Christ, the spiritual economy of the world changed. Christ became High Priest in heaven's tabernacle (Heb. 8:1-3). He desires to connect every human to the Creator-Father by His priestly ministry (Ex. 19:6; 1 Peter 2:5).

The invocation of His name in our priestly ministry provides the opportunity for Him to reveal Himself as alive to an unbelieving world. Jesus said, "Until now you have asked nothing in My name. Ask, and you will receive" (John 16:24).

- *We pray in His name* because through Him we have direct access to the Father.
- *We pray in His name* to honor His sacrifice.

- *We pray in His name* because He came to us from God and now invites us to approach Yahweh as Father, using His name.
- *We pray in His name* because He died and rose again.
- *We pray in His name* because we are promised spiritual treasures in His name.
- *We pray in His name* because we, His bride, have taken His name and we are championing His cause in the earth.
- *We pray in His name* because our new identity is fused with Him—we are members of His body.
- *We pray in His name* in a desire to make our requests consistent with His life's purpose, with what He came to do and with how He lived.

We pray in His name, because no one has ever lived on earth comparable to Him, fully God and fully man. He is love and truth fused together. He has compassion with principle, and principle with love. He is no mere man. No one is in His class. He is incomparable, exalted, above and apart from all other humanity and all gods. "There is no other name under heaven given among men by which we must be saved" (Acts 4:12). God has given Him a name above every name (Eph. 1:21; Phil. 2:9).

He commanded us to pray in His name, not merely as a memorial to Him, but because of the consolidated power represented by His name. Six times in John's Gospel the command is repeated, "in My name" (14:13-14; 15:16; 16:23-24, 26). Jesus is not just one more way to heaven, He is *the* Way (John 14:6; Acts 4:12). If the Father sacrificed His only begotten Son to create one more way among many, He is not a beloved Father to be trusted and adored. Such a father would not be a good father. There is only one way to God, and that is through Jesus, the Christ.

To deny prayer in the name of Jesus alters the Christian faith. It is an attack on the heart of faith. How can there be Christianity without Christ? It is more than another ethical system. Christians have a relationship with the indestructible Christ. Out of the vitality of this relationship, we live. Jesus is more than a good model, He is more than a mere inspiration, He is more than a great teacher. He is God and Savior, our kingly Lord! To deny Him is to deny our faith. To be told that we cannot pray "in the name of Jesus" is the very spirit of antichrist.

## Pray for God to Be Glorified

"Whatever you ask in my name, that I will do, that the Father may be glorified" (John 14:13). When our purpose is to glorify the Father, Jesus will bring all the resources of heaven to bear on our request. "Every answer to prayer," Andrew Murray says, "has this as its object. When there is no prospect of this object being obtained, He will not answer."[33]

God's glory is the end of prayer. It is why Jesus came: "I seek the honor of Him who sent Me" (see 5:44). "Father . . . glorify Your Son, that Your Son also may glorify You" (17:1). Glory comes to those who give glory to God. In a culture where self-interests are the strongest motives behind prayer,[34] the answers will be meager! We are "praying amiss!" To do all to the glory of God requires that we ask all for the glory of God. "These twin commands are inseparable: obedience to the former is the secret of grace for the latter."[35] Richard Foster argues:

> To ask "rightly" involves transformed passions. In prayer, real prayer, we begin to think God's thoughts after Him: to desire the things He desires, to love the things He loves, to will the things He wills. Progressively, we are taught to see things from His point of view."[36]

Jesus was consumed with giving the Father glory, and He has been crowned with glory. If we order our lives to give Christ glory, He will crown us with glory.

## Pray to the Father, the Judge of the Universe

Technically, our prayers are addressed to the Father. We pray to and through Jesus, our attorney-priest who represents us. The Holy Spirit enables us to pray. Prayer, at times, is like a legal petition presented in heaven's courtroom. Only citizens of heaven have access there. Only those whose names are in the Book of Life gain admission. Only those in a covenant relationship through Jesus Christ may appeal to the benefits in the covenant.

In heaven's courtroom, those presenting their claims must pray based on Scripture, consistent with God's holy nature and according to His will. The only way we have a claim on heaven's throne is by our relationship to Christ and our position as bride and believer in the new covenant by His blood.

All court systems operate by the rule of law; so does the court of heaven. Christ did not come to destroy the law of God, but to fulfill it by grace (Matt. 5:17; Rom. 6). Our covenant standing gives us the privilege of prayer, of accessing the throne of God. We file our petitions and place a claim on the storehouses of heaven, based on the finished work of Christ.

## Pray, Submitting to the Will of God

In prayer, we bow. We kneel. We bend our stiff hearts. We humble ourselves. We come with a contrite and broken spirit. Prayer alters our attitude, inviting dependence rather than independence. It engenders confidence, not in the flesh, but in the Spirit. Without prayer, we are proud and self-sufficient, always at arms lengths from God. And "God resists the proud, but gives grace to the humble" (1 Peter 5:5; see also James 4:2-6).

Prayer inverts our passions. We pant for heaven's waterbrooks. We hunger for God. Such Spirit primacy is alien in a fleshly culture. Many prayer efforts today are attempts to get God to agree with us. Real prayer brings us into agreement with Him. Insights come. Sensitivity to the Spirit is heightened. We are readied to be His instruments. "Not my will, but Your will be done." In prayer, we invite God's reign. We plead for the "will of God" to be done in our lives. We invite heaven to invade the earth.

## Pray With Eternal Kingdom Purposes in View

So, we pray always. We live in a spirit of prayer. We pray always according to the Word of God—prayers informed by Scripture. We pray by the enabling of the Holy Spirit, asking for "an anointing" to pray. We pray in the name of Jesus. We pray to the Father, the Judge of the universe. We pray, submitting our requests to the will of God. So we pray always, according to the Word, with the enabling of the Spirit, in the name of Jesus, to the Father, submitting all my needs with Kingom purposes in view. The Scripture teaches us that "God could be approached anywhere but not anyhow (John 4:24)."[37]

# THE DISCIPLINE OF PRAYER

Prayer is the defining factor in the war with the flesh. The "spirit . . . is willing, but the flesh is weak" (Matt. 26:41). The presence or absence of prayer is often the simple difference between defeat or victory. The athlete who believes he can win on chance or talent alone, without the regimen of training necessary to succeed, is deluded. He may win a few amateur contests, but he will not progress far beyond that without the disciplines that sharpen the edge of mere talent.

The exercise of godly habits, including prayer, allows us to enter contests with the flesh and the devil confidently, as fit instruments for God.

At one level, God protects our innocence; and as a David, we slay our Goliath. But God requires us to practice the rigors of warfare without which we will surely fail. Flabby Christians who consistently ask for grace to do what righteous disciplines should do in response to grace will rarely be catalysts for a significant move of God. The absence of the discipline of prayer will manifest in fleshly ways. Conversely, the presence of the healthy discipline of prayer is one of the indicators that we will win the war with the flesh and the devil.

In prayer, we access greater grace in which we are able to stand. Not falling into sin is so often traceable to the quiet time with God that started our day. Grace is not merely the reach of God that compensates for our failures. Grace is the evident power of God that works in us at the moment of the test and allows us to overcome. Grace is the invisible hand that keeps us on our feet, and not merely the merciful hand that gets us up after we have sinned.

Prayer produces saints, men and women whose lives are marked by godly character and who have been graciously enabled to live beyond the grip of sin. This is the glorious promise of prayer and practical living. "Consider!" Paul instructs us (see Rom. 6:11 NASB; Col. 3:5-10 NASB). Challenge the way to see things. A new mind-set is required for the effective Christian. But the change cannot be merely rational. "Now . . . put them all aside," and he names the works of the flesh which must be abandoned and left by the side of the road if we are to continue on salvation's journey. But still more is required.

"Putting off" is followed by the "putting on." "Putting on" alters our thinking more: "Put on the new self who is being renewed to a true knowledge according to the image of the One who created him" (v. 10 NASB). Habitual sin signifies an undisciplined mind. The discipline of prayer lets in the fresh, clean air of heaven that purifies the mind.[38] Francis Paget says, "Your thoughts are making you. We are two men . . . what is seen and what is not seen. But the unseen is the maker of the other."[39]

## Questions for Discussion

1. Have you ever thought about creating a prayer space in your home? Where is your special place of prayer?

2. When you pray, do you "pour out your soul"? Do you empty your cargo—the toxic stuff you have collected in your heart?

3. How do you use your Bible as an aid to your prayer life? Have you ever prayed Scripture?

4. How important is repentance? Why do Christians resist confession of sins when forgiveness is so freely promised? When was the last time you saw a move of God that prompted spontaneous, tearful repentance and reconciliation?

5. What do you think of the idea that Christianity is not merely being "free from" but also "free to"? Are you free to lift holy hands, pray openly, express worshipful love?

6. What would you do if you were asked to pray at some public venue, but told not to mention the name of Jesus?

7. Talk about grace as the safety net for falling Christians, and grace as the empowerment to keep us from falling. What does prayer have to do with grace?

# CHAPTER 3

# Family Prayer

**Foundation Study:** God's Fingerprints on the Family

**Bible Focus:** Deut. 6:1-9

## Central Truth

"You shall love the Lord your God with all your heart, with all your soul, and with all your strength" (v. 5). Our relationship with God is defined by love. It is the primary motive driving all we do. This love consumes us wholly and fully.

## Key Principles

The family is the primary institution upon which God depends for the transmission of faith and values. Our home is to be marked—distinguished as belonging to God—by our conversation, our rituals, our routines, our visual cues and symbols, and our incidental teaching. The goal of parenting is to call out of our children a profound love of God that is lifelong. Only when the faith is transmitted to the next generation are we successful as parents. No other role is more significant than the induction of our children into a personal relationship with God.

## Points of Emphasis

1. The home is the primary means by which faith is transmitted from one generation to the next. Do you agree?

2. Nothing can take the place of parents who demonstrate their love for the Lord. How can parents do this?

3. Deuteronomy 6 suggests we talk about the Lord morning and evening. When walking or resting, God should never be far from the conversational center. What message do we send to our children when prayer and faith-talk happens only at church? Or mealtime? Why is it hard for some people to casually talk to the Lord, praise Him, or live so evidently in His presence?

4. God is not seen as distant. He lives with the family in the home. He is to be a celebrated guest. What could you do to bring your children closer to God? How do parents help their children celebrate God, and not see Him as a distant friend whose house they visit weekly?

5. Around the house, Moses suggests, we should place visible symbols of faith. Coming and going, we are reminded that this home is different. It is marked. Inside is a family that welcomes God and acknowledges Him. The home is identified as a house of faith. What sets your home apart as a house of faith? What might prompt neighbors or visitors to inquire about Christ? Is God in your family schedule at any other time than on Sunday?

6. On the children were symbols of faith. How powerful are symbols? Can we use symbols without assigning to them magical qualities? It is so easy to become idolatrous, to put faith in an object rather than in God himself. So, is there a place for faith-symbols that we might give to children as reminders of our prayers for them and God's love over them?

7. Love is caught! If our children are to love the Lord, is this likely to happen if parents fail to model an undivided heart of devotion to God? How do parents demonstrate their love for Christ and, in so doing, infect their children with the same passion?

## Insights

One of the practices from the life of the patriarchs was the power of blessing. Along with the birthright came blessing. Esau faltered; and in a moment of weakness he sold his birthright, forfeiting the blessing (Gen. 25:29-34). Jacob was no saint, but he saw the generational power of the blessing. Despite his character flaws, he wanted what the blessing would bring. After Isaac blessed Jacob, he could not retract the blessing. This is the power of words: they cannot be recalled or canceled. Esau, a hard man, wept, "Have you not reserved a blessing for me?" (27:36).

The heart of every child longs for the blessing of the father. Sometimes fathers feel inadequate, spiritually deficient. As a result of their own spiritual poverty, they fail to bless their children. But the blessing is not something that comes *from* the father, but rather *through* the father! As people of faith, it is the desire of our Father God to bless His children's children. Every father acts in the privileged position of passing on both generational blessings from godly parents, and the greater blessing of the Father God.

You do not have a right to die until you have held your children close, touched them, prayed for them, wept over them, and blessed them. It may be the most powerful moment in the shared life between a father and a child.

# A NATION ADRIFT

An American minister recently conducted a Bible literacy test on Sunday morning. The results were staggering. In a congregation of 300, many could not identify *Calvary* as the place of Jesus' death. *Gethsemane* rang no bell for 43 percent. *Pentecost* had no significance for 75 percent. Only 5 percent got a score in the range of 90-100. About 12 percent answered 70 percent correctly. Further, 80 percent knew less than half of the answers to simple Bible facts. Does a basic knowledge of the Bible matter? A prison survey of 1,700 inmates found one man from a home with a history of a daily, old-fashioned, family altar. This man was later found innocent and released! One thing was common among the 1,699 other men found guilty of crimes worthy of incarceration: no family altar.

Fifty years ago, multiple voices—the church, the home, the school, neighbors and friends, the business community, government, and more—reinforced the same values. Those value reinforcers are now gone. The number of books used in the public education of our children, when put in a pile, would be 17 feet high. In that pile would be no Bible. There would be no Christian prayer. Conservative Christian faith would likely be persecuted and Christian ideas censored. Christian subjects would likely be disapproved for papers. But the problem cannot be fixed by merely returning prayer and Bible reading to schools.

Families in this nation stopped praying at home long before the privilege of praying in schools was taken away. We've made a great deal about the removal of prayer and Bible reading in school, but the greatest loss is the absence of prayer in the home. Lockyer declares, "True family life is dependent upon family recognition of God."[1] That recognition can't be incidental. It must be intentional.

# Faith in the Home

The Bible says in Deuteronomy 6:1-7:

> These are the statutes and judgments which the Lord your God has commanded to teach you, that you may observe them . . . that you may fear the Lord your God, to keep all His statutes and His commandments which I command you, you and your son and your grandson, all the days of your life, and that your days may be prolonged . . . that it may be well with you, and that you may multiply greatly as the Lord God of your fathers has promised you—"a land flowing with milk and honey." . . . You shall love the Lord your God with all your heart, with all your soul, and with all your strength.
>
> And these words which I command you today shall be in your heart. You shall teach them diligently to your children, and shall talk of them when you sit in your house, when you walk by the way, when you lie down, and when you rise up.

Faith is transmitted intergenerationally, from father to son. The place of transmission and training is not the synagogue or the Temple, or by inference, the church. It is the home. The home has always been the institution upon which God depended for the transmission of faith.

While "sitting in the house" or "walking by the way," when "rising up" in the morning or retiring in the evening, there were conversations about the Lord. Spontaneous faith lessons were to occur. Praise was heard. Sincere prayers were to be prayed. Every day, God was acknowledged. He was never taken for granted, never ignored. Silence does not honor Him appropriately.

In the Christian home, as it was in the Hebrew home, it should be a normal thing for children to hear parents talk about faith. The atmosphere of the home should be filled with audible and visible signs of our love for God. These were not to be formal teaching sessions held four times daily. This was incidental teaching. It was teaching that was as natural as breathing.

Parents who love the Lord openly create an infectious environment in which children catch the faith. Intentional teaching and training are essential. But incidental inculcation of values is even more powerful. If how we live and spontaneously respond to the challenges of life does not reflect deeply held practices, all our intentional efforts will fall flat.

Formal prayer and worship times are important. But it is the flavor of the home that is so radically transforming. It is the diligent love of the Lord, not merely dutiful devotional times. It is having "the words" in our hearts that naturally springs to conversations with and about the Lord while sitting in the house and talking. It isn't what we try to do—it is what we most naturally do! It is the natural bubbling up of our love for the Lord that spills out on every aspect of family life and does so in a way that is natural and not contrived. When we get up, we praise Him. When we walk by the way and notice a sunset, we offer gratitude. When we lie down, we whisper worshipful thanks. When we sit by a child with a fevered brow, we sing prayerfully to the Lord.

Symbols of faith were to be "on your hand" and on your forehead—"between your eyes" (v. 8). The placement of these symbols suggest that faith is to affect our doing and seeing. "On the doorposts of your house and on your gates" were also visible symbols of faith (v. 9). The place and the people who lived there were to be marked as belonging to God.

Such deep spiritual deposits never get away from a child. The book *Grandma, I Need Your Prayers!* has this wonderful story:

> I learned the Lord's prayer at the age of five, sitting on a stool at my grandmother's knee. When she tucked me in bed, she would thank God for the day with a long prayer. In the morning, she'd ask me to say, 'Amen!' to that prayer and she'd start the day, praising the Lord. Whatever came up during the day, she'd stop and talk to the Lord about it, carrying on a conversation with Him as though He was right there in the room. . . . She made God as real as the man next door.[2]

New Testament instruction for transmitting faith is found in Ephesians 6:4: "And you, fathers, do not provoke your children to wrath, but bring them up in the training and admonition of the Lord." This command is specifically for fathers.

A study has indicated that when a mother attends church without a father, the likelihood of the children attending as adults dropped 90 percent. But when a father attends church, even without the mother, the number of children inclined to attend church as adults stayed the same, and in some cases increased. The power of a father's example in faith is profound.[3] Fathers are not to provoke their children to wrath. They are not to relate in a way that irritates or exasperates a child. They avoid provoking negative behavior. Relationships are framed in ways that invite a positive response. This means a father must know the temperament and personality of each child.

The second command is positive. Fathers are to bring their children up in the *training* (KJV, nurture) and *admonition* of the Lord. Our children are our first disciples! The home is God's discipling institution; children are the disciples of Christian parents. The first tool to use in discipleship is *nurture* (training). It involves love, correction, instruction and, when necessary, redirection. *Admonition* means warning and reproof. The Greek word is *nouthesia*—from *nous*, meaning "mind" or "intellect"; and *tithemi*, meaning "to put or place." The idea is to put or place something in the mind. The father helps the child see positive alternatives to life choices. Admonition sometimes says "No," but it also points out the right way!

In American society, we accept the responsibility for the care, basic provision and shelter of children. Sadly, we have allowed the state to assume responsibility for the education of them. Further, we have asked the church to assume the responsibility for the moral education of our children. This was never the intent of God. It is not what the Bible teaches.

# THE FAMILY ALTAR

## The Tradition of the Family Altar

Family worship was once the norm for Christians. In *Nead's Theological Works*, an 1850 publication, we find, "Heads of families ought to observe prayers with their families, mornings and evenings. This is generally termed 'Family Worship.'"[4] Through the centuries, Christians have gathered twice a day for corporate prayer: morning and evening. This pattern goes back to the morning and evening sacrifice in the Old Testament Tabernacle. Morning prayer begins the day, tuning our hearts to heaven.

Evening prayer closes the day, committing the day to God, confessing any sense of failure and celebrating the day's God-moments. It allows us to enter the rest of God as we retire.

A hundred and fifty years ago, family worship was common. Christian families prayed together daily. Home altars and worship centers were common. Guests participated. Worship consisted of Bible reading, prayer, and singing. The family altar acknowledged dependence on the invisible guest of the home—God himself. It said, "We are not alone!" On special occasions, in good times and bad, and in seasons of transition and triumph, the family gathered to pray. When something good happened, they would stop and offer prayerful thanks. When danger threatened, they prayed. Family prayer doesn't have to be long—ten to fifteen minutes may be sufficient. Consistency is more important than length.

## Changing Times

Abraham was a sojourner, but he took his faith and his altar with him. His tent might have been pitched on different turf, but his altar anchored him to the same God. "Abraham was a man of the altar," Matthew Henry said. "Wherever he had a tent, God had an altar . . . sanctified by prayer. He erected his own altar that he might not participate with idolaters in the worship offered upon theirs."[5]

The family altar differentiates us from the pagan world around us. It identifies our children with the precepts and presence of God. It is a compass and an anchor. In premodern times, the hearth, where the food was prepared, was "the focus" of the home. From it, the family was fed. At it, the family was kept warm. Out of it, light shone into the darkness. Around it, in the evening, after supper, the family gathered for prayer. The fireplace was a reflection of the ancient altar, which was always associated with fire.

In the twentieth century, family worship began to experience a marked decline. Christian education took place in the Sunday school. Prayer and worship occurred at church. As the industrial revolution intensified and fathers left the home for work in factories, a strange view of men emerged in America. Men were worldly, women were pure. Men were breadwinners *in the world,* women kept the hearth *at home.* Men traded their roles as spiritual leaders in the home for providers outside the home.

Today, the home is often little more than a place where we sleep and keep our stuff. Many families do not share meals together. Such practices do not create healthy families that model biblical purpose.

The greatest need for prayer in the Christian community is in the Christian home. The disappearance of the family altar has come simultaneously with the breakdown of the family and the culture war on our youth. Barna says we are only churching 3 percent of "Generation X." We are losing our own kids to the world. The absence of prayer in the home is more damaging than its absence in the church. In fact, when prayer is something strange and foreign to daily life, we have created something very different from New Testament Christianity.

## Renewing the Practice of the Family Altar

In a survey involving 1,000 churches, parishioners were asked, "Why does the church exist?" Eighty-nine percent responded, "To take care of my family's and my needs."[6] The church is not about us, it is about God. We have everything upside down in our me-first culture. The church cannot care for personal and family spiritual needs in a one-hour, once-a-week experience.

Without the family altar, Christianity is in danger of becoming a just-for-Sunday activity. The family altar marks the home.

It invites conversation about the God we serve. It centers us daily. It defines who we are: a family belonging to and representing God. It differentiates us from the world around us.

Many of our homes have nothing that sets them apart from nonpracticing Christians next door, except for a few religious items. The family altar is a reminder that we are the people of God. Prayer at and around it creates unforgettable expressions that anchor us for a lifetime.

Some traditions publish books to use as prayer guides. You may choose a less formal approach. What is important is to develop some plan—systematic readings, regular prayer-focus points, Christian development issues. Remember also that prayer was never intended to be a monologue. God talks to us, too. Teach your children to hear from God through Scripture and through the Holy Spirit's gifts.

## A Physical Space

Everyone needs a place to fix broken things, to cook and sew, to laugh and sleep. The Christian family needs a place to meet with God—the family altar. Some Christian traditions encourage families to construct an altar for family worship. The place does not have to be fancy. It should be noticeable enough to provide focus and marked as special. At the altar the family will experience their most vital activity—prayer, reading Scriptures, and family worship. Every family altar should be unique to the family, but certain features will be common.

Some altars are designed, like the Tabernacle, to face the rising sun. This is a symbolic, daily reminder of the coming of Christ, the Sun of Righteousness (Mal. 4:2). Some altars have above them a wall-mounted shelf and under that a small table or dresser covered with a decorative tablecloth. On the shelf or the table is a cross, candles, an open Bible, prayer aids, and / or anointing oil.

Family worship should be a natural part of family life and never a burden. The appointment with God should involve the whole family. When guests are present, keep your appointment and invite their participation. If your children have friends over, tell their parents, "This is the evening we have family worship! Would you mind if your child joins in?"

## Couples Praying Together

Every husband and wife should pray together daily if possible, and not less than weekly. A cup of coffee in the morning combined with a morning prayer is a good way to begin the day. Add a devotional:

- Read Scripture together. Read through the Bible together in a year.
- Select a book to study together.
- Pray together regularly for your children and grandchildren. Call them by name. Pause over each name and give the Holy Spirit an opportunity to impress your heart and mind.

## The Christian Difference

In 2004, George Barna released a report that found no difference in the divorce rate of Christians and non-Christians. Additional research indicates that there is more to that story. For couples who attend church regularly, the divorce rate drops by 35 percent. That's significant.

A University of Chicago survey revealed that 75 percent of the Americans who pray with their spouses reported marriages that were "very happy." Those who prayed together were more likely to respect each other, discuss their marriage goals together, and, in a surprising find for the University, report high levels of satisfaction in the area of couple intimacy.

New data indicates that when a couple receives premarital counseling, and not only attends church regularly but takes faith home and prays together, the probability of divorce is one in 39,000. Church attendance is good—it produces a modest drop in divorce; but praying together pulverizes divorce. This is the power of faith, and of practicing faith together.

## The Prayer Difference

Liz and Tom's marriage was in trouble. "It was very dark. There was no love there. Alcohol had come in," Liz said. Tom added that, "I think that bringing the Lord into our lives" and "praying together" saved the marriage.[7]

Doug and Beth's marriage was in trouble. Three children, two job changes, and two 1,000-mile moves had stressed the relationship to the breaking point. Beth, in a bold attempt to save the relationship, asked her husband, Doug, to begin praying with her. Doug was not a Christian. In fact, he was nonreligious, a self-proclaimed man of science. But Doug felt that if saying prayers with Beth could save the relationship, it was worth a try.

"I soon found that praying together brings out a real sense of selflessness and humility," Doug says. "When you're praying for each other, not just yourself, you're focused together and speaking from the heart on a whole different level. I would never have predicted this for us, but it really works."

"As bad as any problem may seem at that moment," agrees Beth, "prayer always helps us see beyond it. It doesn't have to be a long-drawn-out Scripture reading, just a few minutes a day. When we pray, it brings another level of honesty to our conversations. I think it's the most intimate thing you can do with another person." Now they pray together every night.

Julie's marriage was also strengthened as a result of prayer. "It's pretty short and not at all scripted," she says about the giving of thanks before each meal. "We just join hands and let it rip. Whether we're asking for forgiveness or giving thanks, saying it out loud holds a lot of power. Most marriages require a ton of faith. You've got to believe that somehow the two of you are going to make it through things. You've got to believe that you're being blessed with this person."

## Prayer Implications for Couples

When a couple prays together, they are following the example of Christ in prayer. This provides a safe and regular forum in which to invite God into personal and marital struggles. The individuals hear the concerns of their spouse, especially spiritual and relational burdens. They develop a capacity for greater openness with one another.

The bond between them becomes stronger—not just physical attraction, but a more holistic bonding takes place that is both emotional and spiritual. Their unity increases. They find themselves consistently on the same page about issues they face. They invite God to intervene in their lives and in the lives of their children. And He does.

Couples who pray about their family, their business concerns, their finances, their giving to the Kingdom, and God's work report miraculous results from prayer. The number of disagreements declines. Couples are taking their stresses to God in prayer, looking to Him for answers. As a result, they tend to be more patient with each other, see things from an eternal perspective. They lay a spiritual foundation for a spiritual legacy for their children.

## Prayer Goals for Couples

Beyond praying for one another and for the needs of family and home, a couple might do the following:

- Pray daily for their children.
- Pray for unsaved family members and friends, work associates, and neighbors.
- Designate at least one day a week or month to pray for your pastor and other spiritual leaders.
- Pray regularly for some ministry of the church.
- Adopt at least one missionary for prayer. If you can't send financial support, pray for them.
- Adopt an unreached people group. Make it your prayer project. Pray until you have heard that God has raised up a missionary to go and reach them, then pray for them.
- Adopt a parachurch ministry for prayer—one that works with local schools, the homeless, unwed mothers, seniors, prayer and unity causes in the community.
- Pray for political leaders. Choose a mayor, a city councilperson, a state legislator, a national legislator, the president or a member of his staff. Send the person you choose a note, saying, "I'm praying for you."
- *Create a couples prayer triad* with two other couples. Adopt mutual projects for prayer. Confer with one another monthly. Share information about the people, ministries, and causes you are praying about. Get together once a quarter for an evening of prayer and sharing. Pray for one another's kids.
- Pray for others, particularly for the kingdom purposes of God. Be missional in your praying. Pray with harvest eyes.

# OUR JEWISH PRAYER HERITAGE

The Jewish pattern is a family faith experience each week. Every conservative Jew knows where he would be on Friday evening when he was growing up. By sundown, the preparations would have been made, the table adorned, the candles lit. Prayers would be offered, songs sung. There would be recitations—repetitive acts—for children.

Theology and mystery are laced into the ritual. The litany is rich with variety. Each family member has a role. This weekly repetition marks the home as belonging to God, and each member a part of the covenant family. Through 1,900 years without a homeland, a holocaust, and countless experiences of repatriation, these people survived and tenaciously held to their identity.

The regular experience of seeing Dad and Mom pray, of singing and praying together as a family, marks Jewish children with a distinctive identity. They never get away from their roots. These weekly faith and prayer ceremonies anchor them as a people. Even nonpracticing Jews recognize their Jewishness. Perhaps our aversion to ritual has inoculated us from such practices. Or it may have been the years in which the church steered away from Jewish roots and substituted Christianized pagan holidays. Whatever the reason, there would be value in recovering home-based faith celebrations which express the biblical calendar.

## The Feast Days—Faith Celebrations

Old Testament feast days contained the Gospel message in code. The feasts were more than cultural festivals, they were prayer events. Combining a party with prayer is unusual for us, but the feasts also contained solemn moments. The altar was a busy place on such occasions. There, the nation met with God. What are the feasts and their themes all about? What are the encoded messages? This panoramic scope of the Gospel message is the eschatological calendar of God's work in a time-space world. What would it look like for a family to use this annual calendar to reinforce God's redemptive story? To teach and pray around each theme. To have special family festivals and celebrations. Each feast has a theme:

- *The Passover* pointed to Christ the Lamb, the Redeemer.
- *The Feast of Unleavened Bread* pointed to the need to purify our homes and set ourselves apart as the people of God, freshly redeemed, separated from the world as Israel was separated from Egypt.

- *The Feast of the Firstfruits* pointed to Christ, the firstfruit of the resurrection from the dead. The first sheaf of the spring harvest was offered to God in the Temple in thanks for the coming harvest. Dead seeds, buried in the ground, had come to life. The risen Christ promises life to us. His resurrection is a prophecy of our resurrection. We must die to live.
- *The Feast of Pentecost* looked to the giving of the Law and the coming of the Holy Spirit. In the New Testament, the Spirit writes the Law on our hearts and guides us into truth.
- *The Feast of Trumpets* looks forward to the return of Christ and the last-day events.
- *The Day of Atonement* looks to the Great Day of the Lord.
- *The Feast of Tabernacles* looks to the reign of God on the earth.

# A Family Faith Calendar

Add to these, Christmas and Resurrection Sunday (which often coincides with Passover and the spring feasts). Using such an annual calendar, every year would provide the opportunity for parents to reinforce basic theological truths. Touching these themes and praying around them in season, linking one with the other, begins to build in the mind of the child the continuity of message, the power of the story into which he has been called to live. It is a story that has not reached its ending. It is not over.

We too are players on the stage of this wonderful drama. Such a view of life calls us to live beyond ourselves. It invites our children into something larger than life. It helps them see generational continuity. They begin to see themselves as extensions of God's past and His certain future. Suddenly, they are in a line with all the great biblical characters being a part of their past. Their family has been expanded. They are sons of Abraham by faith.

The great cloud of witnesses who line the balcony of heaven are members of our extended family. Our children are moved to play their parts in carrying the drama forth into the next generation—and doing so prayerfully.

## Let the Children Pray!

Children long to pray. They are natural pray-ers! Tom Bisset, in his book, *Why Christian Kids Leave the Faith,* found that something had happened which had not allowed them to explore inconsistencies that troubled them. They did not see faith working in "real life" ways. So they never personally owned the faith! They had conformed to standards to avoid parental confrontation, but they had never been deeply transformed. Still, Bisset says:

> God is everywhere . . . always seeking His own. Walking away from your faith is not simply a matter of washing your hands of God. . . . He is ceaselessly calling His own back to the Father's house. It does not matter that these wanderers refuse to listen . . . will not attend church or that they become silent when the conversation turns to spiritual things . . . if they refuse to read the Bible or pray. They cannot escape from the God who is everywhere and who is always speaking.[8]

A grandmother with two three-year-olds said:

> I get up early in the morning to pray and read the Bible. . . . When the grandchildren wake up and come out of their bedroom, I'm in my chair praying. They snuggle up with me as I finish. I'll read a few verses or pray aloud. . . . They learn this is the normal way I start my day.[9]

Dale Evans was thirty-five when she came back to Christ. She learned Christian principles at the feet of her grandmother. One of her ancestors had been jailed for street-preaching. Incarceration couldn't stop him—he preached through the jail-cell window to people below. "His genes are strong in me!" Dale said, "His heritage is partly responsible for my forthright declaration of Christian faith in the midst of a show business career, even at the expense of a contract."[10]

# THE TRANSFORMING POWER OF PRAYER

Henry Grady was the editor of the *Atlanta Constitution*. He became a household name and a potent political power, famous for his use of the phrase "the New South." He was considered a possible presidential running mate in the 1888 election. He died at the young age of thirty-nine. Grady is credited with one of the three great orations in American history. The first was by Patrick Henry, at Williamstown; the second, by Abraham Lincoln, at Gettysburg; and the third, by Henry W. Grady, at New York.

Before giving the oration, Grady had been stranded by a sudden thunderstorm. Bridges were washed out and roads were not crossable. On the hillside, he spotted a small cabin. Knocking on the door, he found a humble family who gave him shelter. Sitting at their table, he watched them offer thanks. Later, he observed the father with the family Bible, reading to his children. Each member of the family prayed around the room. The father turned to Henry and asked him to close in prayer. Grady, whose profession was that of a wordsmith, recalled that his mouth turned to paste. There were no adequate words. The simplicity of faith and the peace of that home overwhelmed him. He stuttered and stammered.

Lying on a straw mattress that night in the darkness, he asked himself what made this country. Was it the massive structures in Washington? Was it the natural beauty of the continent? Was it industry or initiative? Was it freedom granted by the Constitution? No, he concluded. It was what he had just witnessed—the decency of common people whose lives were rooted in faith and a healthy fear of God.

The next day, he altered his plans and headed for Athens, Georgia. He spent nearly two weeks with his mother at his childhood home. He felt his own hold on the Christian faith was lessening.

"Mother," he said as he took her in his strong arms, "I have come home to spend a week with you. . . . I want to go back to the old days and be your boy again. Tell me the old stories about the stable, the shepherds, the wise men, the star, the teachings of Jesus and His desire to make the world better, His crucifixion, His ascension. Tell me how He wants me to be a good boy."

After Grady returned to his roots and renewed his faith in what he saw as the roots of our greatness as a nation, Grady went to New York City and gave what is regarded as one of the great speeches in the history of the nation.

## Questions for Discussion

1. What visible symbols do you have in your home that testify of your faith?

2. Why do you think our culture has abandoned the family altar? How could you take steps to restore it in your home?

3. How could Christians adapt the Jewish idea of weekly worship (the Sabbath eve) for a weekly family meal and worship experience?

4. Talk with your spouse about setting prayer goals for the two of you. Make a list.

5. What do you think about the idea of creating prayer triads with other Christian couples and families? What would a quarterly family prayer fellowship look like?

6. What about the idea of creating an annual family-faith calendar? Some families celebrate "spiritual birthdays" as being as important as natural birthdays.

7. What do you remember about the family altar in the home in which you were raised? Were you ever impacted in an unforgettable way by a praying parent?

# CHAPTER 4

# Intercession and Evangelism

**Foundation Study:** The Critical, Strategic Middle

**Bible Focus:** Luke 11

### Central Truth

Jesus came to the earth . . . to pray! More than preaching and teaching, more than healing and caring, His ministry was prayer. He began and ended His ministry in prayer. He prayed early in the morning and late into the night—sometimes through the night. He prayed before and after momentous experiences. God "wondered," Isaiah 59:16 says, "that there was no intercessor." Jesus came to fill that void. On the cross He prayed . . . and split humanity down the middle—with belief on one side and scoffing on the other. Everything He did flowed from His connection with the Father by prayer. The most important thing Jesus taught His disciples was to pray! *Lord, teach us to pray.*

### Key Principles

We see prayer in our culture as a means of acquisition. Petition is a wonderful privilege afforded the believer, but it is not the heart of prayer. We so often want to be "on the end" of a blessing or breakthrough. Here, Jesus seeks to move us from the end to the critical and strategic middle, the place of the intercessor. It is this place Jesus came to reclaim, the place that was lost in the Fall. It is the place that the Evil One illegitimately claims. The middle is uncomfortable. Here, we find ourselves besieged by needy people for whom we have no provision. As we pray, God meets their needs. The greater blessing is always in the middle, more than on the end.

## Points of Emphasis

1. Luke says of Jesus, "Now it came to pass, as He was praying in a certain place, when He ceased, that one of His disciples said to Him, 'Lord, teach us to pray'" (Luke 11:1). What would it have been like to hear Jesus pray? The disciples were so captivated by His praying that their request was "Teach us to pray"! Do you think we pray like He prayed? Hebrews 5:7 says Jesus prayed "with vehement cries and tears." How often did He pray that way?

2. The prayer Jesus taught His disciples is both a model to be prayed and a pattern for prayer principles. How often do you pray that prayer? Have you ever used it as a template for prayer?

3. Not once do you find *me, my,* or *I*. Instead, you find *our, us,* and *we*. We were never to pray for ourselves exclusively. Praying effectively requires praying for others. Do you agree?

4. This prayer begins and ends with God. It begins with the Kingdom—the rule and reign of God. In Matthew's version, it also ends with the Kingdom: "For Yours is the kingdom and the power and the glory . . ." (6:13). Do your prayers begin and end with God, or with yourself?

5. Do your prayers grapple with the rule and reign of God in your life situation? So often our prayers focus on our narrow slice of pain. Pray about the in-breaking kingdom of God. This prayer seems designed to stretch us beyond ourselves.

6. This prayer sees God in personal terms—Father! It is not a closed transaction with God, however. He taught us to pray for our own daily bread, forgiveness and deliverance. This prayer demands that we assume an open and transforming posture. God will give us daily bread, but He also wants to transform us into givers. Forgiveness is not so much the

goal of God as it is to make us a forgiving people. Recognize the difference between prayer as a transaction with God, and prayer as a means by which God transforms us.

7. This is prayer "from the middle!" Too often, we pray from the end. Here Jesus calls us to pray not just for ourselves, but for others, too. He wants us in the middle, acquiring blessings and passing them on. We pray for others *and* for ourselves.

8. In the parable that follows Jesus' prayer, notice how He emphasizes persistence (Luke 11:5-8). The lesson seems to be that we give up too easily, that "the friend with plenty" would respond if only we would persist.

9. *Ask, seek,* and *knock* are all in the present tense (v. 9). We are to "keep on" asking, seeking, and knocking. Prayer is not an event, it is a process. These words in the imperative mood mean we are to keep on asking with intensity, passion, and an I-can't-be-denied attitude. Yet, this is not about asking something for ourselves. It is about asking for one who does not have a relationship with the friend with plenty! Prayer, then, is the means by which we introduce our friends in need to the One who can graciously satisfy their inner hunger.

10. The resistant friend with plenty is redefined. He is more than a friend; He is our Father. The parable turns from comparison to contrast. If a friend with plenty will meet a need at midnight because of sheer persistence, "how much more" will your heavenly Father meet such a need?

## Insights

All over the world, God is using prayer as means of opening the eyes of unbelievers. As Christians give "the gift of prayer" to people in need, God reveals Himself as alive and loving. The call is for the believer to move from the end of prayer to the strategic, critical middle. It is a call to stand between the Father and those in need who don't know Him. Never able to meet such needs and feeling inadequate, we often run from the uncomfortable middle. And yet, if we could meet such needs, people would look to us as savior and deliverer instead of the Lord. God brings people to us whose needs are overwhelming. Simply pray and love them . . . and He will reveal Himself.

# PERSISTENT INTERCESSION

Dr. Ray H. Hughes is a legend in Pentecostal circles. He was the president of Lee University and, subsequently, the denomination's School of Theology. He was general overseer of the Church of God three times, head of the National Association of Evangelicals, and chairman of three Pentecostal World Conferences. He represented the Pentecostal Movement to Presidents Reagan, Carter, and George H. W. Bush, often in meetings in which Billy Graham represented Evangelicalism.

But he may have never been saved apart from intercession. He often told the story of the afternoon he ran home from school and dashed through the front door. Picking up his ball glove and heading out the back door, he heard a captivating sound from upstairs. Drawn to the music of prayer, he slowly climbed the steps. The sounds became clear words. The voice was that of his mother. She was pleading with God, "Save my boy, Ray!"

Like something driven deep into the heart, Ray Hughes never escaped that moment. Like a deer who continues to run a short distance after the battle with the hunter is over, his running from God was near its end. The intercessory spirit that makes prayer a merciful net had captured him. The arrow of God's love expressed in his mother's voice had gone deep into his heart. God would not let him go. Prayer harnessed him, and God through him touched a world.

# PRAYER EVANGELISM

The highest calling of prayer is communion with God. But the noblest use of prayer is intercession, especially when we pray for the lost. Sometimes we can't pray for ourselves. That's when we need an intercessor. Sensitivity in prayer will never allow us to focus only on our own needs.

Praying for those under stress and pressure around us is so important. Hold up the hands of Christian leaders through prayer. Ultimately, the great role of intercession is not representing others before God, but advocating for God in behalf of others. It isn't capturing the pain on earth, but the pain in God's heart *for* the earth.

*We must move from asking God to take care of the things that are breaking our hearts, to praying about the things that are breaking His heart.*[1]

## The Gift of Prayer

In a culture that is increasingly resistant to the Gospel, prayer may be the greatest avenue to make people aware of God's gracious love. Give the gift of prayer to the unsaved. A pastor shopped occasionally at a store in New York. As far as the pastor knew, the store owner was not a Christian. The location of the shop in a high crime area was not the most desirable. One day he called the pastor in frustration: "My store keeps getting robbed, and there are drug dealers in front of my place day and night. Pastor, what are you going to do about it?"

Pastor Alex asked, "Why don't you call the police?" The shopkeeper confessed that he had called the police, but they had told him there was nothing they could do about the situation. "So," he said, "I am calling you." In a nation increasingly out of control, our only hope is the intervention of God—but the church is unprepared to respond.

At first the pastor was baffled. Then God reminded him of the powerful impact of on-site prayer. "I'll tell you what. Let me come down to your store once a week with a group, and we will pray that God will intervene. Is that okay?" The store owner agreed. That Thursday afternoon, shoppers heard a strange sound coming from the back room of the store. In the subsequent weeks, a few asked the owner what was happening "back there!" Pastor Alex recalls, "We prayed in earnest that God would protect the store and that the drug dealers would be dealt with."

Within four weeks, four drug dealers were arrested. Two families who shopped at the neighborhood store began to attend Pastor Alex's church. The store owner saw the hand of God. Prayer should never be a thing we keep to ourselves. Intercession is a gift. We use our relationship with God for the good of others; and God, who desires to touch through us, begins to do just that.

## The Three "Greats" of the New Testament

Sadly, only 9 percent of adults can correctly identify the term *Great Commission* as the command of Christ to tell His story to the world. Amazingly, 84 percent don't have a clue as to what the term means.[2] "Go into all the world and preach the gospel to every creature" (Mark 16:15). A paraphrase could be understood in this way: "As you go about in the earth, proclaim Christ wherever you are. Share Jesus. Tell the story of His good news and His love!" All of us are called to do this.

The Great Commission needs to be wrapped in the *Great Commandment* to have maximum impact. The Great Commandment is this: "'You shall love the Lord your God with all your heart, with all your soul, and with all your mind.' This is the first and great commandment. And the second is like it: 'You shall love your neighbor as yourself'" (Matt. 22:37-39).

Something happens in conversations with people who feel we love them. Love changes the relational environment. Love breaks down resistance. Love is irresistible. Truth without love is like bitter medicine without sugar. Truth is the fact of the Gospel; love is the reality of the Gospel. Truth is the head talking; love is the heart touching. Truth is propositional; love is incarnational. The Commission and the Commandment have to go together.

Paul gave us another "great." It is sometimes called the *Great Commitment*:

> I exhort first of all that supplications, prayers, intercessions, and giving of thanks be made for all men, for . . . all who are in authority. . . . For this is good . . . in the sight of God our Savior, who desires all men to be saved and to come to the knowledge of the truth (1 Tim. 2:1-4).

Prayer aimed at community leaders and the unsaved is the key to getting them saved. It is also the key to a safe community, according to Paul. In Colossians 4:3, Paul suggests that prayer opens doors. In 2 Corinthians 4:4, he indicates that the "god of this world" blinds the minds of those who do not believe. Even believers need prayer to heighten spiritual perception. "Open my eyes, that I may see wondrous things from Your [Word]," the psalmist declares (119:18).

Intercession means praying the blinders off. It is the means by which we ourselves are changed into credible witnesses. The more we pray for the unsaved, the more we find God loving them through us. Prayer changes us, and it works to open the hearts of our friends to the reality of God's presence. When they sense God's love, those previously closed to the Gospel and the reality of God are suddenly open to consider truth. Prayer, the Great Commitment, empowers us to love at the level of the Great Commandment. Love, then, paves the way for the Great Commission, the effective sharing of the Gospel. Prayer evangelism is the root of all successful evangelism.

## Intercession and the Lost

The Great Commission is not optional; it is a command. Love infects us. We have to talk about Christ. He saved our soul. We cannot help but whisper His name. To see the world dying and withhold life-giving support is criminal. How can we keep quiet? Prayer strengthens us for the task. Prayer opens the hearts of those for whom we are praying. Prayer creates the connection that allows the sharing of faith to take place.

Intercession is the call to stand between God and the lost. It is the greatest tool we have for the task of completing the Great Commission. Barna notes that "privatized faith is common in contemporary America because it is so congenial with a highly differentiated society. Restricted largely to spheres of family and personal life, it encroaches very little into the public world, which Americans increasingly define as off-limits to religion."[3]

A pastor at a prayer summit prayed: "I thank You, God, for Rachelle Wilson. I remember the morning I went to work, pushed my time card into the clock, turned to Rachelle, and said, 'I have something to tell you.' She looked at me and said, 'You got saved this weekend. Now I can check you off my list.'" Rachelle was a Christian, but she was more. She was an intercessor, a woman of prayer. She had found a way to combine work and ministry.

Rachelle kept the time clock for the company. As a result, she had the task of regularly reviewing all the names of the workers at her company. Without any fanfare, Rachelle prayed for the salvation of every worker as she regularly reviewed the names. She called the names out to God silently, asking Him to save them, to change their lives. Almost immediately after the pastor finished, another prayed: "God, I also too want to thank You for Rachelle Wilson." As sinners, both men had worked for that company at different times. Having never met before, they discovered, in the context of this prayer event, not only their common work background but a common connection with a faithful woman who had prayed for their souls. Now, both were in ministry, serving churches in the same city, because of a faithful intercessor.

## Intercession, God Loving Through Us in Prayer

Love constraints and prayer lengthen the arms of love, reaching beyond human capacity. Paul declared, "Since the day we heard about you, we have not stopped praying for you and asking God to fill you with the knowledge of His will through all spiritual wisdom and understanding. And we pray this in order that you may live a life worthy of the Lord and may please Him in every way: bearing fruit . . . growing . . . being strengthened" (Col. 1:9-11 NIV).

Susan Gaddis said, "The intercessor is an advocate, one who represents or pleads the cause of another."[4] William Law notes, "Nothing makes us love someone so much as praying for them."[5] Luther called prayer "climbing into the heart of God." There is perhaps no greater way to impact a person's life than to consistently pray for him or her.

Leonard Ravenhill declares, "To stand before men on behalf of God is one thing, to stand before God on behalf of men is something entirely different." Andrew Murray says:

> Time spent in prayer will yield more than that given to work. Prayer alone gives work its worth and its success. Prayer opens the way for God Himself to do His work in us and through us. Let our chief work as God's messengers be intercession; in it we secure the presence and power of God to go with us.[6]

This is the premier role of the intercessor. Stepping into the gap, we stand before the Lord! And we stand in behalf of the other party—perhaps someone or someplace deserving of and about to receive discipline. The intercessor stands between God and the offending party (Num. 16:47-48). Intercession calls a truce. It pleads for mercy. It builds a wall around the guilty. It seeks to protect the guilty from God, from His judgment and from His wrath (1 Sam. 2:25).

Stepping into this gap is precisely what God wants us to do.[7] The *delight* of prayer is found in our communion with God. The *duty* of prayer, though not without delight but driven by a sense of mission, is found in intercession.

You cannot intercede properly until and unless you spend time in communion. Communion with God is the cause behind intercession. Having experienced the rest and peace of God (communion), we project that very rest and peace toward people and places where it is absent. We invite the Prince of Peace to assert His rule in troubled hearts, homes, neighborhoods, and nations.

The soul that is won is first claimed by prayer. Where the Spirit brings liberty to a life, invariably an intercessor has tracked through the rubble, declaring by prayer the power of God's grace in the person or place.[8]

## Intercession and the Character of God

Prayer is an indication of our faith, not only in God's *ability* but in His *character*. The child who screams for parental assistance doesn't analyze the parent's capacity to respond to the situation. He appeals only to compassion. Crying out to God is the instinctive sense we have within us about the nature of God. He is a God of love, good and full of mercy.

Why would we pray to a God who did not love us? The absence of a clear conviction of God's love impedes prayer. It is the enemy of faith, the antidote to hope. Love says, "He cares, and He is good!" Specifically, "He cares about me, and if I pray, He will respond with grace and mercy." Faith in God's *power* is never enough. It is faith in His *character* that drives us to "cry out" to Him. Robert E. Speer said:

> The evangelization of the world depends first of all upon a revival of prayer. Deeper than the need for men . . . aye, deep down at the bottom of our spiritless life is the need for the forgotten secret of prevailing, worldwide prayer.[9]

## Intercession and the Heart of God

At Gethsemane, Jesus' intercessory cries rose to the Father. His *compassion* (the Greek word is *splagchnon*) spills out on the ground through tears of intercession. Intercession should overflow with deep inward affection, with God's tender mercies thundering up and out of our inward parts. When our innermost beings are filled with His *splagchnon*, the oppressed are set free. Christ, as God, prayed and wept for humanity. The Father responded in unity with the Son and "arose to judgment, to deliver all the oppressed of the earth" (Ps. 76:9). "God heard their groaning, and God remembered. . . . God looked . . . and God acknowledged them" (Ex. 2:24-25).

Epaphras prayed "fervently" (Col. 4:12). Bonar uses the phrase, "with strong, great wrestling, souls are won."[10] Paul asked the Romans to "strive together" in prayer (Rom. 15:30). The word is "agonize" (*agonizomai*), from which we get the word *agony*. It is the idea of "throwing the whole soul into praying."[11] In earnest prayer, we do not merely *say* a prayer. The *whole of our being* goes out in prayer. We are consumed by the prayer experience. Such prayer is exhausting. Praying is one thing, but crying out to God with holy desperation is another. It was when Israel *cried out* to God that He heard them. Throughout Scripture—from Israel in bondage to blind Bartimaeus—crying out with holy desperation puts God's people on the cusp of breakthrough. E. M. Bounds says:

> To say prayers in a decent, delicate way is not heavy work. But to pray really, to pray till hell feels the ponderous stroke, to pray till the iron gates of difficulty are opened, till the mountains of obstacles are removed, till the mists are exhaled and the clouds are lifted, and the sunshine of a cloudless day brightens—this is hard work, but it is God's work and man's best labor.[12]

When you were a child and found yourself injured or frightened, you *cried out*. Nothing is more motivating to a parent than the scream of a desperate child. Diminutive mothers are transformed into warriors in behalf of a distressed child.

# THE STRATEGIC POSITION OF INTERCESSION

The first formal prayer in the Bible is in Genesis 17: "Oh, that Ishmael might live before You!" Abraham cried (v. 18). The plea is in the form of a prayer. It is the cry of a father in behalf of his child.[13] John Welsh spent eight of every twenty-four hours in prayer. David Brainerd rode through the American wilderness, praying as he went. John Wesley changed the face of England with bold and earnest prayer.[14] Jonathan Edwards recalls:

> I rode out into the woods . . . as my manner had been, to walk for divine contemplation and prayer. I had such a view that for me was extraordinary of the glory of the Son of God . . . this continued for an hour; and kept me the greater part of the time in a flood of tears and weeping aloud. I felt an ardency of soul to be what I know not otherwise how to express, emptied and annihilated; to love Him with a holy and pure love; to serve and follow Him; to be perfectly sanctified and made pure with a divine and heavenly purity.[15]

Intercession is not simply an activity, it is a strategic position. It reclaims the dominion granted to Adam in the beginning when he was placed in the middle, between God the Creator and all of creation. We do not presumptuously aspire to this position. Jesus, the last Adam, has recovered the strategic middle which Adam forfeited. This embattled turf is what Jesus came to the earth to reclaim. It is what Lucifer illegitimately purports to own. Intercession is always in the strategic middle, between God and disconnected men and women.

## Intercession, the Uncomfortable Middle

In Luke 11:1, the disciples, after hearing Jesus pray, asked, "Teach us to pray!" Robert Murray McCheyne said, "If I could hear Jesus praying for me in the next room, I should not fear a thousand devils."[16] What follows the familiar Lord's Prayer in Luke 11 is a parable. There are three players in the story. One is a traveler who comes into a city after dark. Without housing or food, he remembers a friend who lives there. He locates him and knocks on his door. He is welcomed warmly, but there is a problem.

The host can provide housing for the night, but he apparently recognizes hunger in the eyes of his traveling friend. The host has no bread in the house, however. This urgent need demands immediate attention and cannot wait until tomorrow. But it's midnight! Even Wal-Mart is closed. The third player is a friend of the host who always has plenty. The host goes to his friend and insists he arise from his bed, answer the door and lend him bread. This well-supplied friend with plenty is the most resistant. The story is designed to emphasize our need for persistence in prayer. Will the friend in the uncomfortable middle be denied? Does he have a strong enough relationship with the friend with plenty to sustain such an intrusion at midnight? Will he give up and let his friend in need go hungry?

The friend in the middle will not be denied. He is as intense as if he were the hungry one. This is the true spirit of intercession. We pray as if we are the person we are representing in prayer. Their need becomes our need. Intercession places us in the uncomfortable middle. All of us have unsaved friends. Sometimes they call at midnight . . . and a call after midnight is rarely a good call. They turn to us in crisis looking for support in the time of a personal storm.

God knows, in placing us in the middle, that we can't meet their need. The middle position demands humility. Many people shrink back from the middle and deliver their needy friends to a Christian professional: "Here, you are trained. Deal with this. Help them." But God wants every believer in the middle. We pray, and He does the miracles. We make the introductions; He reveals Himself as alive. We prefer the end position. That is, we want to be on the end of the blessing, with someone more spiritual in the middle. So much of American Christianity is about receiving—receiving a blessing or breakthrough from the Lord. But the greater blessing is never on the end. It is the blessing that comes from being in the middle.

## Intercession, the Need for Persistence

Emphasizing the need for persistence in intercession, Jesus sweetened the dynamic. "If a son asks for bread from any father . . ." (Luke 11:11). A *son*? A *father*? No longer are we a friend going to a resistant friend with plenty. We are *sons*, going to the *Father* with plenty, and He is never reticent to answer. Luther said, "We pray for silver, but God often gives us gold instead."[17] We give up too easily. "If you . . . know how to give good gifts to your children, how much more will your heavenly Father give the Holy Spirit to those who ask Him!" (v. 13).

Ask, seek, knock; you will receive, you will find, and doors will be opened. All three terms are in the present tense. *Keep on* asking until you get an answer. *Keep on* seeking until you make a discovery that leads to a breakthrough. *Keep on* knocking until you disturb heaven and God opens a doorway. Not only are these terms in the *present tense,* they are in the *imperative mood.* Ask with intensity. Seek relentlessly. Knock forcefully. This is not sissy praying. Not your typical prayer meeting. This is vigorous prayer. These are weighty expressions of hunger and need. They are compelling pleas, animated yearnings, driving prayers, urgent appeals. Pray reasoned, but craving petitions.

Our prayers lack such intensity. The result is that our words *say* we are desperate for God, for friends and family to know Him, for a great awakening in our culture; but our lack of persistence and our less-than-intense mood show we are willing to live without the requests we say we so desperately need. Without persistent, imperative praying, our unsaved friends will remain lost. If we are not praying for them, who is?

## Intercession, the Problem of Interference

In intercession, the middle position, we grasp the hand of God and touch the world through prayer. It is not uncommon in such moments to have, simultaneously, a holy and unholy encounter— to experience peace *and* sense of conflict, to see victory and defeat *together*. This clash of light and darkness is the influence of both heaven and hell on our world. An intercessor steps into a vortex of swirling powers. Sometimes it is like being on the edge of a thunder cell. Explosive and stormy discharges of disruptive energy are possible. This demands we pray with an awareness of the schemes of the Evil One.

Prayer is focused Godward, but it often gains the attention of the Evil One. Flashes of warfare are not uncommon before, after, and during seasons of intercession. We cannot allow ourselves to be conditioned into avoiding intercession to escape such warfare moments. Prayer is for such moments. Scripture warns that we are to be aware of the devil's "devices" (2 Cor. 2:11; see also Eph. 6:10-18). Prayer is an alert system that heightens awareness of a coming storm or prepares us for it. Nothing takes God by surprise. Because prayer's warning system nurtures obedience and assures our hearts of certain triumph, Satan hates nothing more.

The book *The Kneeling Christian* reminds us: "Satan laughs at our toilings and mocks our wisdom, but he trembles when we pray." It is not our power, but God's mighty hand to enter the fray that is a power with which Lucifer cannot contend. The devil dreads nothing so much as prayer!

Today, much emphasis is on spiritual warfare; but the goal of intercession is reconciliation, not spiritual warfare. The focus of intercession in some circles has degenerated to warfare tirades against the darkness. God has not called us to warfare. When an intercessor steps into the critical, uncomfortable middle, warfare is inevitable. That place is occupied illegally by Satan in his attempt to separate man from God. But the inevitable spiritual conflict cannot be the primary focus of the intercessor. The Scriptures say, "Better to have wisdom than weapons of war" (Eccl. 9:18 NLT).

The role of the intercessor is to connect, through prayer, the lost or displaced person to God and God to that person. The goal of intercession is reconciliation. The work of the Evil One is to distract, to cause us to miss our purpose. He creates confusion among intercessors regarding their role in the middle, or he attempts to displace them completely. We must stay in the middle, sometimes fighting the hornets, yet making our prayers of reconciliation the main thing. We pray, holding tools of edification in one hand and the sword in the other. We don't want to fight. We are not called to fight. We are called to build up, to edify, to strengthen, and to intercede from our place on the wall.

## Children as Intercessors

In an old YMCA-type building in Argentina, there were about fifty children, ranging from age four or five to their teens. They led worship, shared testimonies, and ministered to some international guests. A six-year-old boy told how a girl had stolen his lunch money. He prayed for her, and the next day she brought his money back and apologized. Then he led her to Jesus! Unbelievable!

After formal worship, the children moved through the audience to pray for those in attendance. As these children turned toward the audience, they didn't just go systematically. They looked and waited for instructions from the Lord. Then they went to specific people to pray for them. The prayers were simple, yet powerful. Many of them simply praised God, saying repeatedly, "*Recibelo, recibelo!*—Receive it, receive it!" All over the earth, children are being raised up as intercessors. It is an unprecedented and unbelievable phenomenon.

The Children's Global Prayer Movement brochure features some of their comments:

- Aaron, 11: "I'm a world-class intercessor now."
- Tom, 6: "My awesome prayer power works!"
- Breanna, 4: "I'm a mighty prayer warrior, thank you."
- Jenna, 8: "My desire to pray isn't strange. It's from God!"
- Jesse, 5: "Praying is more fun than toys."
- Kelly, 9: "It's time to pray, not play; weep, not sleep."[18]

Esther Ilinsky of this Movement says, "A new breed of children—righteous seed—has emerged on the world scene. These are world-class intercessors—World Shapers, I call them. They are praying for their peers, the two billion children twelve and under who live on earth."[19]

Peter, quoting Joel, declared, "Your sons and your daughters [your children] shall prophesy" (Acts 2:17). The promise, Peter declared, is for your children! Tragically, we have offered the entertainment of children's church rather than introduction to life in the Spirit. When Jesus rode into Jerusalem, the children cried out, "Hosanna to the Son of David!" (Matt. 21:9). Religious leaders objected then, as now, to such religious fervor from children. Jesus said, "Out of the mouth of babes and nursing infants You have perfected praise" (v. 16).

Today, Jesus is saying again, "Permit the children to come to Me!" Corporate prayer should never be a childless event. God wants intergenerational prayer. Children can teach us so much about simple faith and earnest prayer.

## Intercession and Spiritual Power

D. L. Moody's church burned during the 1871 Chicago fire. In 1872, he visited England to raise money to rebuild the church and to listen to great English preachers. One Sunday he agreed to minister at a church in London. The experience was a disaster. Moody said he had never had such a difficult time preaching in his life. A deadness seemed to grip the service. Relieved that the service was over, he realized he had to preach there again that night.

That evening, however, the atmosphere was different. There was an air of expectancy in the packed church. Moody said, "The powers of an unseen world seemed to have fallen upon the audience." At the end of his message, he gave an invitation for people to acknowledge Christ as Lord. He was astounded when five hundred people stood. He told everyone to be seated, thinking they had misunderstood. He repeated the invitation. When a large number responded again, he did it a third time to be sure only the sincere came. All five hundred went to the vestry to pray to receive Christ. Night after night, he continued to preach an unscheduled meeting. A revival had started in that church. What had happened?

One woman left the service that Sunday morning and casually told her invalid sister that a visitor named Moody had preached that morning. The invalid sister turned ashen. "Mr. Moody from Chicago?" she inquired with surprise. The invalid sister had read about Moody and had been secretly praying for God to send him to London to preach in that very church. "If I had known he was going to preach this morning, I would have eaten no breakfast and spent the whole time he was preaching in prayer for him. Now, sister, go out of the room, lock the door, and send me no dinner. No matter who comes, don't let them see me. I am going to spend the whole afternoon and evening in prayer!"

Paul recruited the Thessalonians to serve as an intercessory support team. He said: "Pray . . . that the Word of the Lord may speed on (spread rapidly and run its course) and be glorified (extolled) and triumph" (2 Thess. 3:1 Amp.). As powerful as the principles are, the seeds must be carried on the wind of the Spirit. The Spirit comes by prayer.

Moody had stood in the pulpit that morning alone without intercessory support. That night, the ice chamber he had experienced in the morning met fire. It was all because of the prayers of a bedridden saint who was interceding. Moody heard about the woman and recruited her as an intercessor for the rest of her life.[20]

## Questions for Discussion

1. If it is true that the great work of pre-evangelism is prayer, who is now praying for your lost family members and friends?

2. Are there people you know whose only regular contact with a committed Christian is you? What role do you think prayer might play in their salvation?

3. Have you ever considered the trio called "the three Greats?" How do the three together form a perfect strategy for evangelism?

4. To whom could you give the gift of prayer?

5. What would happen in your church if you adopted the Moravian principle, "No one works unless someone prays"?

6. What is the difference between praying and crying out to God? Do you allow yourself to become intense in prayer?

7. Do you think the Children's Global Prayer Movement may be predictive of a coming revival?

## CHAPTER 5

# The Ministry of Prayer in the Church

**Foundation Study:** The Prayer Ministry of the First-Century Church

**Bible Focus:** Acts 1–5

### Central Truth

The Holy Spirit descended on a praying church. The early church was born in prayer (Acts 2). They called the first disciples to prayer (v. 42), and they themselves continued in prayer. They prayed in homes and at the Temple. They prayed in the streets and they prayed privately. Out of their prayer sessions flowed the power of God. That power impacted a city. The entrenched establishment was no match for a praying church. They had no answer to the miraculous presence of the risen Christ.

### Key Principles

There were two kinds of miracles in the Book of Acts. First, there were the obvious signs and wonders, healings, and interventions of God. But the less noticeable type of miracle was the transformation of the nature of the church itself. Believers were in unity. A spirit of grace and unity prevailed. The character of the church, evidenced by love and sacrifice, created a community unlike the push and shove of the religious establishment around them, and even more distinct from pagan notions of faith. The character of the relationships was as miraculous as the glaring miracles. Glory and beauty belong together. What message is sent when the blazing glory of God is disconnected from the beauty of holiness? Supernatural power and supernatural fruit are by the same Spirit!

## Points of Emphasis

1. Why do we have revivals that end up producing little lasting effect?

2. Notice the character of the miracles in the Book of Acts—how are they connected to evangelism, to the mission of the church?

3. Notice the location of the miracles in Acts 1–5. Many are in the streets. What would a revival look like in which the power of God was demonstrated not only in churches and convention halls, but in the streets?

4. We seem to think that a miracle will convince everyone—did they in these passages? Is it possible that miracles only bring people to a place of decision, and then they must acknowledge or deny the truth of the miracle worker, Christ?

5. What would happen to you if you were told not to pray or speak the name of Jesus? If you were caught in the middle of a mighty move of God that divided your community and pressure was brought on you to disassociate yourself from the church to save your job or position—what would you do?

6. In a nation increasingly hostile to conservative Christ-centered faith, what would empower a church to remain firm? What was the source of the boldness of the Acts church? Are you a bold believer?

7. When questioned about his association with Jesus, Peter denied he knew Him. Fifty days later, he challenged an entire city. What changed him?

8. The authorities crucified Jesus, even after witnessing His miraculous power. The disciples saw the scenario play out.

They knew it could end in the same way for them. What emboldened them? What would it take for us to stand up against a corrupt culture and call for a great awakening?

9. Do you think your church is a Book of Acts kind of church? Why or why not?

10. Are you a Book of Acts kind of Christian? Why or why not?

## Insights

Pentecostals often put emphasis on the awesome power of God, but flashes of God's glory in the darkness are an intended beacon in the night. They are to draw people to the living Lord and to His bride representative, the Church. Power is not enough. Paul told the Corinthians that tongues without love is only noise. Jesus said a life full of the prophetic, even with power manifestations and mighty works, was like a house without a foundation, if it lacked fruit (Matt. 7:15-27). Fire without fruit is not true Pentecost. It is a prescription for apostasy.

# THE CHURCH AND POWER

J. Vernon McGee said: "According to my humble judgment, the greatest need of the present-day church is prayer. Prayer should be the vital breath of the church, but right now it is gasping for air. One of the great Bible teachers of the past said that the church goes forward on its knees. Maybe one of the reasons the church is not going forward today is because it's not in a position to go forward—we are not on our knees in prayer."[1]

E. M. Bounds says:

The great lack of modern religion is the spirit of devotion. We hear sermons in the same spirit with which we listen to a lecture or a speech. We visit the house of God just as if it were a common place, on the level with a theater, the lecture room, or the forum. We look at the minister of God not as the divinely called man of God, but merely as a sort of public speaker. We handle sacred things just as if they were the things of the world. Oh, how the spirit of true and genuine devotion would radically change all this for the better![2]

A "feeble, lively, showy religious activity" can never compensate when the "spirit of genuine, heartfelt devotion is strangely lacking."[3]

The Book of Acts explodes with miraculous power. Jerusalem is on its heels, reeling from the impact of the resurrected Christ, who is alive by the Spirit and working through the church. In the first five chapters, Luke seems to layer one miracle feature after another. There are eight miracles mentioned: Acts 1:9; 2:1-4, 43; 3:1-10; 4:31; 5:1-11, 12-16, 19. In both 2:43 and 5:12-16, numerous miracles may have occurred. Notice how the first five interweave with prayer:

| *Prayer* | *Miracles* |
|---|---|
| A command to tarry precedes . . . | the miracle of the Ascension (1:4, 9). |
| As the church obediently obeys Christ and persists in prayer . . . | the fire falls, the wind of heaven blows and they are filled with the Spirit (2:1-4). |
| The church continues in prayer; | signs and wonders abound (vv. 42-43). |
| Peter and John go to prayer; | God heals at the Temple gate (3:1-10). |
| The church gathers for prayer under threat from the officials . . . | in response to the Spirit (4:31). |

- The miraculous Ascension is coupled with the command to wait prayerfully in the Upper Room (Acts 1:4, 9).
- The Holy Spirit comes to a room full of united, praying believers (2:1-4).
- Signs and wonders happen in the context of a praying church gladly receiving the Word (2:41-43).
- The lame man is healed as Peter and John head to a prayer meeting (3:1-10).
- After threatened if they mention the name of Jesus, the church gathers for prayer and the room trembles (4:31).

Here is prayer on top of prayer. These are powerful demonstrations of God's presence coming from prayer. This is the

Acts church. When church growth slowed and internal strife manifested, the correctional strategy was a reinvestment in prayer. "We will give ourselves continually to prayer and to the ministry of the word" (6:4). When this happened, division was healed and church growth resumed. Years ago the order was given that Christian Protestants could no longer hold meetings in the city of Osaka, Japan. The officials resisted all attempts to rescind the ban. Two Christian leaders did the only thing they knew to do—pray! A Japanese girl entered the room to call them to supper, and fell under the power of prayer.

The wife of a leader did not understand the delay, and went to seek her husband. She too fell under the spirit of intercession. That night, in defiance of the order to cease the meetings, they opened the mission hall. As soon as the meeting began, God came down. Two sons of city officials went to the altar that night and were saved. The next morning, the leaders got word, "Go on with your meetings, you will not be interrupted." The daily newspaper reported in boxcar letters—"THE CHRISTIANS' GOD CAME TO TOWN LAST NIGHT!"[4]

## Prayer and Witness

"What does this mean?" asked the Jerusalem crowd in response to the Holy Spirit so evidently manifested. It means, Peter explained, that Jesus who was crucified is not dead. His soul was not left in the grave (Acts 2:27). He is "exalted to the right hand of God" (v. 33). The empowerment is proof that He is alive. Authorities who had sought to silence His message and stop His miracles were now faced with a dilemma. Instead of one man or even twelve, they had 120 behaving like Jesus.

"God has made this Jesus . . . both Lord and Christ" (v. 36). He promised to return in a way the disciples would see Him, but the world would not. He said the Holy Spirit "dwells with you and will be in you" (John 14:17). Because of this He said: "He who believes in Me, the works that I do he will do also; and greater works than these he will do, because I go to My Father" (v. 12).

How do you fight a ghost? How do you destroy the indestructible? Emboldened by Jesus' resurrection and the indwelling Spirit, the disciples were now as fearless as He. They talked like Him, acted like Him, did miracles like Him. The Holy Ghost changed them in more ways than one. Christ was evident in their proclamation, but there had also been a second incarnation. Christ was in them—in love and truth, as well as in power.

True Pentecost demands Christlikeness. The greatest sign and wonder is a transformed church. If people see supernatural power but fail to find supernatural fruit, they will only be disillusioned. Signs and wonders are advertisements of the fact that Jesus is alive. They are invitations into Jesus, into the body of Christ, into a new way to live.

## Prayer and Character

Miracles are not the only signs and wonders. The character that emerges in the church itself is miraculous. The disciples continued steadfastly in teaching, learning, and growing. Their *koinonia* was exceptional; it was a family-like fellowship. They shared. They prayed together in the homes of one another. Praise resounded in the streets. Daily, people were joining the movement. The Holy Spirit had changed the character of the church itself. There was an absence of clamor for position. Humility now characterized them.

| *Miraculous Character* | *Miraculous Power* |
| --- | --- |
| They were all with one accord in one place . . . (Acts 2:1). | Suddenly there came a sound from heaven, as of a rushing mighty wind. . . . There appeared . . . tongues, as |

of fire. . . . They were all filled with the Holy Spirit. . . . The multitude came together (vv. 2-4, 6).

Then fear came upon every soul, and many wonders and signs were done. . . (v. 43).

Now all who believed . . . had all things in common, and sold their possessions and goods, and divided . . . as anyone had need. . . . Continuing daily . . . in the temple, and . . . from house to house . . . with gladness . . . praising God and having favor with all the people (vv. 44-47).

Those who believed were of one heart and one soul; neither did anyone say that any of the things he possessed was his own (v. 32).

Nor was there anyone among them who lacked; for . . . possessors of lands or houses sold them, and brought the proceeds . . . and laid them at the apostles' feet (vv. 34-35).

And with great power the apostles gave witness to the resurrection of the Lord. . . . And great grace was upon them all (4:33).

Ananias, with Sapphira . . . sold a possession. And he kept back part of the proceeds . . . and brought a certain part and laid it at the apostles' feet. But Peter said, ". . . Why has Satan filled your heart to lie to the Holy Spirit. . .?" Then Ananias, hearing these words, fell down and breathed his last (5:1-3, 5).

So great fear came upon all. . . . And through the hands of the apostles many signs and wonders were done among the people. . . . And believers were increasingly added to the Lord.

... A multitude gathered from the surrounding cities . . . bringing sick people and those . . . tormented by unclean spirits, and they were all healed (vv. 11-12, 14, 16).

Peter and the other apostles . . . said: "We ought to obey God rather than men." They had called for the apostles and [beat] them. . . . So they departed . . . rejoicing that they were counted worthy to suffer shame for His name. . . . They did not cease teaching and preaching Jesus (vv. 29, 40-42).

[Authorities] laid their hands on the apostles and put them in the common prison. But . . . an angel of the Lord opened the prison doors and brought them out, and said, "Go, stand in the temple and speak" (vv. 18-20).

John Newton once said: "If two angels were to receive at the same moment a commission from God, one to go down and rule the earth's grandest empire, the other to go and sweep the streets of the meanest village, it would be a matter of entire indifference to each which service fell to his lot, the post of ruler or the post of scavenger; for the joy of the angels lies only in obedience to God's will.[5]

E. M. Bounds declared:

> Humility retires itself from the public gaze. It does not seek publicity nor hunt for high places, neither does it care for prominence . . . it is given to self-depreciation. It never exalts itself in the eyes of others nor even in the eyes of itself.[6]

Jerusalem witnessed a miracle even more profound than the street miracles—a people of one heart and mind, caring and sharing, praying daily, loving their enemies, living in grace, and giving witness to the reality of another world and the resurrection of Christ from the dead. They had been freed from *things*. They gave. They liquidated their assets to finance the first great surge of the Gospel. They became a sharing, caring community committed to the mission of Christ. *Agape* love flowed. Fellowship was sweet. Joy was abundant. It seemed that the whole city wanted to become members of the church.

In our day the tendency is to emphasize supernatural power and not supernatural character. Paul, in the discussion about Pentecostal gifts (1 Cor. 12–14), introduces the topic of *agape*. The essence of character is unconditional love. Power manifestations without character are confusing. Fire minus fruit is not what the Pentecostal church experienced in Acts. Judgment on Ananias and Sapphira is testimony to that demand. Truth must be a lifestyle, not a stated doctrine.

Without integrity our message is hollow. As Dr. Joe Aldrich, of the pastor's prayer movement, was fond of saying, "The gospel rides on the beauty of the transformed church. We don't have the message. We are the message." What we proclaim, we must incarnate. Our lives speak louder than our words. Jesus is the message in the Book of Acts. "Silver and gold I do not have, but what I do have I give you: In the name of Jesus . . ." (3:6).

- *Acts 1:11; 2:20.* Jesus is coming back.
- *Acts 2:22-24.* Jesus is a man of miracles, wonders, and signs; crucified, yet alive.
- *Acts 2:32-33.* Our purpose is to give witness to His resurrection, His exaltation, and the supernatural coming of the Spirit as evidence.
- *Acts 2:36.* Jesus is the King, the Lord and Messiah, sitting at the Father's right hand.
- *Acts 2:38.* Since this is true, sinful men must repent.
- *Acts 3:6.* His name has healing power.
- *Acts 3:13-16.* Jesus, the Prince of Life, was crucified but has now been glorified by the God of Abraham, Isaac, and Jacob.
- *Acts 4:10.* Healing is in the name of Jesus.
- *Acts 4:12.* Salvation is only in the name of Jesus.
- *Acts 4:18-20.* Silence about Jesus is impossible in view of the things seen and heard.
- *Acts 4:26-30.* When the whole nation lined up against them, prayer was offered for boldness to speak the name of Jesus as a witness to His life.

The church understood its role was to *give witness* to the resurrection of Christ. The theme of *witness* emerges in chapters 1-5:

- *Acts 1:8*: "You shall be witnesses."
- *Acts 2:32; 3:15; 5:32*: "We are witnesses."
- *Acts 4:33*: "With great power the apostles gave witness to the resurrection of the Lord Jesus." They are no longer intimidated by the crucifying power of the Romans or the authority of the religious establishment. They boldly offer their witness.
- *Acts 2:12-14, 36*: Peter stands up and boldly answers the accusations.
- *Acts 3:4-7*: They boldly pray for needs in the name of Jesus.
- *Acts 3:11-16*: Peter attributes the miracle of the lame man to Jesus, and asserts that it is proof of both the resurrection and glorification of Christ in heaven.
- *Acts 4:29, 31*: When censored for speaking in Jesus' name, they prayed for boldness to continue to speak despite the threats.
- *Acts 5:1-3*: They boldly confront compromise in the church, even if it is a wealthy and influential couple such as Ananias and Sapphira.
- *Acts 5:29*: When threatened by authorities, they declare their ultimate allegiance to God rather than man.
- *Acts 5:42*: Although beaten, they did not tone down their activities. Daily, openly, and publicly, they continue to preach and teach about Jesus.

This boldness comes from power through prayer. Prayer invites an anointing that demonstrates to a watching world that Jesus is not dead. Still, the underemphasized miracle in the Book of Acts is the transformation in the lives of the believers and the community that was cradled in love and defined by truth. That community—holy, humble, unified, full of the Spirit—was a miracle. We need a miracle that transforms the character of the contemporary church and makes us Christlike, loads our branches with love, joy, peace, longsuffering, kindness, goodness, faithfulness, gentleness, self-controlthe fruit of the Spirit (Gal. 5:22-23).

We need a revival that makes us gracious without compromising truth and causes us to *walk* truth as much as we *talk* truth. If America is going to see revival, it must first see Christ in a transformed church. If America is to repent of its many sins, it must first hear the church repenting of its sins. Judgment, as we learn from Acts 5, begins in the house of the Lord. When unsaved friends and families see us weeping about the condition of our lives before the holiness of God, they might say to themselves, "If the righteous scarcely can be saved, where does the sinner and the ungodly stand?" (see 1 Peter 4:17-18).

We will do more to promote conviction of sin by our response to God's holiness than from attempting to coach a sinful culture into repentance. Our faces, tear-stained over what worldly friends might consider slight sins, and our conscientious desire to please God should cause them to say, "If he needs to repent, I need massive change in my life." In the bright light of God's holiness, our righteousness is always dingy gray. Holy people are humble people.

## Prayer and Unity

Nothing tends more to cement the hearts of Christians than praying together. Never do they love one another so well as when they witness the outpouring of each other's hearts in prayer.[7]

Stephen Olford said, "I came to the conclusion that the two outstanding conditions for revival are unity and prayer."[8] J. Hudson Taylor declared, "The spirit of prayer is, in essence, the spirit of revival."[9] Billy Graham said there were three things that brought revival—prayer, prayer, prayer. Prayer connects the Church with its Head, the Lord Jesus Christ (Col. 2:19). Jesus

Christ alone is able to fill His church with His own life and power. He alone is able to take immediate control of His church and run it from heaven by His Spirit.

The Church is more than a community of doctrine, it is a community of life and love in union with our Lord himself. We can meet with Him and talk to Him in prayer. His church began as a prayer meeting (Acts 1:14), and it is sustained in prayer. Just as children share life and love with their parents, so the church family should share life and love with Christ. Life is tied together by the gift of grace, but this tie must be nurtured. It can be neglected and even severed. A parent who has lost the love of a child is left hurt and empty. The unresponsive church grieves God in the same way. The church at Ephesus neglected its first love. Christ warned it to repent or He would remove the light from its midst (Rev. 2:4-5). The Laodicean church became lukewarm, and Christ said He was ready to spew it out of His mouth (3:16).

Three kinds of churches exist: (1) churches that pray when there is a crisis; (2) churches that have a prayer ministry among other ministries; and (3) churches that seek to bring prayer to the center of every ministry—to everything the church strives to do and be. They want to become a house of prayer for the nations.[10] But prayer cannot be merely a program in the church. It is the third church we seek to emulate.

The prayer ministry cannot be a department among other departments. There cannot be a choice: "If you sing or join our choir, if you teach or are a part of our Christian Education program, if you love youth and work with our young people . . . oh yes, if you like to pray, we have a prayer ministry." Such an approach is doomed to failure. A model for prayer ministry is needed that seeds prayer into every department of the church until you have a praying staff, praying elders, praying youth leaders, praying nursery workers, and praying families.

Everything we do must be bathed in prayer.[11] The whole church and every believer must be called to prayer. Every minister should know that if the prayer meetings are neglected, all his labors are in vain. Unless he can get Christians to attend prayer meetings, all else he can do will not improve their state of spirituality.[12] Jesus not only said His house was to be a house of prayer, it was to be a house of prayer *for the nations* (Mark 11:17). This means prayer moves the church beyond itself, to touch the world.

# THE FOUR CRITICAL ELEMENTS

In establishing a prayer ministry in the church, four elements are critical.

## 1. At-Home Daily Prayer

No level of church prayer can replace daily, personal prayer. If the church is a praying church, the people have to be a praying people. Public prayer can't replace private prayer. Corporate prayer can't replace personal prayer. The two are connected. At-church praying cannot replace at-home prayer.

## 2. The Church at Prayer

We learn to pray by praying. It is more caught than taught. Nothing can replace being in the middle of a passionate prayer meeting. Listening to others pray, blending our voices with theirs, being infected with their passion, sharing their burden for the lost—we catch the spirit of prayer. Like taking coals of fire from the altar, we carry prayer fire home to the privacy of our own prayer closet. A church that has intercessors with hot hearts will always have an altar full of prayer fire. Coming together for prayer will eventually ensure that our home altars glow red with passion for the lost and a love for the Lord. Soon we find ourselves coming to the public altar bringing fire with us. Others will catch our heart fire. A revival spirit will grow. Back and forth, between our home altars and the church, we move. We are not successful in prayer ministry until we have established personal, at-home daily prayer in the lives of our members, evidenced by churchwide prayer events full of humble, but passionate, people of prayer. You must not have one without the other.

*The Church's Prayer Ministry*. Charles Swindoll lamented a letter he received as chancellor of Dallas Theological Seminary. A student wrote in appreciation for his education. He confessed that when he came, "he was deeply in love with Jesus Christ; but when he left, he had fallen more in love with the biblical text . . . he left loving the Bible more than he loved his Savior."[13]

Prayer brings Jesus back to the center of the believer's life! Sadly, our churches become "houses of preaching" instead of "houses of prayer." Frank Lauback charges, "Evangelical Christianity is lost unless it discovers that the center and power of its divine service is prayer, not preaching."[14] Prayer enhances preaching, and preaching should drive us to prayer.

Yet, as Frederick Heiler noted, "Not speech about God, but speech to God, not the preaching of the revelation of God, but direct intercourse with God is, strictly speaking, the worship of God." George Buttrick got it right: "Corporate prayer is the heart of corporate worship."

The Reformation sought to ground the church on objective truth. It made the pulpit central. Buttrick says, "When the Book is made central, prayer may become an appendage of scribal interpretations. When preaching is made central, prayer . . . may become only an introduction and conclusion to the sermon. The heart of religion is in prayer . . . prayer must go through the rite, Scripture, symbolism, and sermon as light through a window."[15] Oswald Chambers declared, "Prayer does not equip us for the greater works, prayer is the greater work."[16]

*Praying Corporately.* Many congregations have never learned to allow the Holy Spirit to move them along together in an unhurried manner, just waiting in prayer. This is a model: One prays, then another. A season of quiet comes. One has a word, another confirms it. Prayers are offered, each following the other, as if everyone was reading from the same script. The many voices become one, corporately learning and listening in prayer. In such moments, the Spirit comes. There is no program, no agenda, no script. The church has gathered to meet God . . . and He shows up.

Other people pray in ways you and I would never pray. This is why we need to hear one another pray. You express my heart with language I did not have. You are bolder and more vulnerable before God than I would have been. You touch something in prayer that resonates in me, that rattles my soul, making me wonderfully uncomfortable. In unhurried seasons, we find others praying our thoughts. In these times of vulnerability and transparency, an honest hunger for God, coupled with genuine repentance and humility, allows the Spirit to pierce the hardest heart. Tears come. Brokenness follows. We are all in the presence of a holy God. The pursuit and spiritual yearning of one feeds the longing in the heart of another. The capacity for humility in one is a quiet and convicting indictment of the arrogance in another. We are "iron sharpening iron." Yet, all this happens in a way that avoids conflict and confrontation. Such prayer is not a mere transaction with God, it is transformational. "The only way up, is down."[17] Performance-based Christianity is out; authenticity and genuineness are in.

While the heart of prayer is communion with God, that is not all of prayer. It involves *intercession*—prayer for others; *petition*—prayer for our own needs; and *thanksgiving*—a humble gratitude that stimulates faith by a regular review of God's gracious history in our lives. Thanksgiving is sometimes a discipline. It wakes up a cold heart. It systematically surveys the past and looks for traces of God's intervention. It marks the path we have taken and signs of God's hand at work in providing and directing, in protecting.

*Praying With Variety.* We are to pray "with all kinds of prayers" (Eph. 6:18 NIV). A good prayer ministry demands variety. Don't allow the prayer life of the church to get into a rut. Pray "with all prayer." Pray with others. Pray aloud at the same time. The fervency of multiple voices lifted to God all at once, like a symphony, is a component of passionate Pentecostal praying that the entire global church is now increasingly embracing.

Yet, in American Pentecostal churches the practice is waning, if not dying. Such prayer is rich with intensity. It is ardent and fiery. But it is not the only way to pray. What we sometimes call "corporate prayer" isn't corporate. It is individuals, each finding a place and praying in the same room aloud together. That is a legitimate and passionate context of prayer. But corporate prayer is different. It puts us all on the same page, on the same topic, praying in the same direction. We need to learn to pray with *all* prayer:

1. **Concert prayer.** Everyone lifts their voices together, praying aloud, as a symphony.

2. **Directed praying.** A focus for prayer is offered, followed by five or ten minutes of prayer. This is followed by a second focus and another short season of prayer. This deliberate process continues until a variety of needs have been considered. Allow time for openness to the Holy Spirit on any matter in order for

the prayer concern to be thoroughly explored. We rush through prayer needs. We simply repeat the need to God with bowed heads and closed eyes, but that is not praying. Good prayer explores a matter in consultation with God.

3. **Small groups.** Each group focuses on a specific need.

4. **Prayers of agreement.** Each person prays in succession, building and loading into the prayers that came before. It is praying as the Spirit leads.

5. **Waiting prayer.** Allow the operation of the gifts of the Spirit. Pray, then wait on a word from the Lord. Pray again, employing a scripture. Rely on discernment from the Holy Spirit. Pray until, by the gracious working of the Spirit, you have reached an end and you sense a breakthrough.

6. **Pastoral prayers.** The pastor offers prayer and the congregation allows him to intercede in their behalf, likely silently agreeing.

7. **Silence.** This is the experience of the holy hush of His presence. No one speaking. No tongues and interpretaion. No prophetic words. Only the piercing voice of the Spirit speaking into each heart.

8. **Congregational prayers.** Several people pray, one after the other, as the rest listen and agree.

9. **Prayers of thanksgiving.** This is prayer for the specific acts and blessings of God.

10. **Prayers of praise.** Focus on the character and nature of God, rather than on His acts. He does what He does because of who He is.

11. **Covenant prayers.** Give voice to His love for us, and for our love for Him. These prayers reaffirm our covenant and express our commitment.

12. **Prayers of repentance.** They reflect our pursuit of character before His holiness.

13. **Intercessory prayers.** Pray for the lost, for unreached people groups, for kings and nations, for the peace of Jerusalem, for family and friends, for pastors and Christian workers, for those in authority, for our cities and counties, for regions and states. Pray for neighbors and work associates, for brothers and sisters in Christ, for the persecuted church, for businesses that bless the community, for enterprises that do harm.

Pray for those stricken with disease, for the oppressed and forsaken, and for those in prison or on probation. What is needed in the church is a "culture of prayer." The goal should be for the entire church to embrace prayer as the norm![18] Here are some additional ideas to move prayer toward the center of church life:

1. Pastors, staff, and other leaders must **model prayer.** The disciples became men of prayer because Jesus was a man of prayer. The Acts church became a praying church because the 120 apostles and lead laypersons were praying people.

2. Establish a regular **churchwide prayer meeting.** Emphasize its importance. Mix time for personal prayer and corporate prayer. Direct the various prayer points for any given evening.

3. Create a **prayer room** in the church facility. Make it accessible seven days a week. Schedule prayer team members to be present and use the room. Open it to all.

4. Appoint a **prayer leadership team.** Have enough members on the team to cover the key areas of nurturing personal and family prayer; networking and training intercessors; integrating prayer into every ministry of the church; proliferating prayer groups; managing prayer needs and rapid-response prayer teams; leading prayer counselors/altar workers, healing teams, pastor's prayer partners, prayer evangelism, and the coordination of the prayer room or center.

5. **Call the men to prayer.** Teach and emphasize the family altar, prayer with wives and children, the power of blessing, and the role of priestly leadership in the home.

6. **Identify intercessors.** Train them. Team them. Debrief them. Direct them.

7. **Pray the sanctuary.** Bathe the sanctuary in prayer. Prayer-walk every foot of your facility. Invite God's presence.

8. **Sponsor a School of Prayer—regular training on prayer.**

9. **Enlist the whole church to join the "Pastor's Prayer Team."** On the day of the month corresponding to their birthday, have them take their place on the wall.

10. Do **prayer walks** and **prayer missions** to push prayer out into the harvest field.

11. **Establish a "wailing wall."** Post pictures and names of friends and family who need a closer relationship with Christ. Weep at the wall. Ask God to reveal Himself to loved ones.

12. Keep **prayer literature and resources** flowing into and through the congregation. Focus on materials that support and enrich the personal and family prayer experiences.

13. **Emphasize answers** to prayer.

14. **Vary the prayer experiences.** Introduce new ways to pray. Introduce tools for enriching the church prayer life, and personal prayer.

15. **Proliferate prayer groups.** Organize a prayer group, small in size, for and around every burden and cause. Train the leaders. Monitor their effectiveness.[19]

# 3. Identify Intercessors

The third critical element for a church at prayer is to identify the intercessors. If anyone is praying at home daily, it is the intercessors. They are also the first people who will show up for churchwide prayer events. The mobilization of intercessors is always a great way to begin a prayer ministry. Every believer is called to intercession. Yet, there are those who have a special burden for the role, even a special anointing to do the work of intercession. Most churches have never identified those people. Tragically, intercessors are ignored and often marginalized. Nothing will move the prayer process forward faster than mobilizing the intercessors. They always have "prayer fire" in their hearts. Here are some action steps:

*Identify the intercessors.* Call them together. Spend an evening with them. Appreciate them. Enlist their support. Most of them are eager to be officially engaged as "watchers on the wall."

*Train them.* Don't assume that intercessors naturally do all things perfectly or even understand the workings of prayer. Some intercessors, due to the absence of any training in this area, have terrible theology. Teach them. Expose them to balanced prayer theology and practices.

*Team them.* Intercessors tend to be loners. The "night wall" is a lonely place. Team them not just to pray together, but to collaborate, to share, to jointly adopt various prayer needs. Create networks of communication among them. Use the teams to confirm the "impressions" they sense from the Spirit.

*Debrief them.* If intercessors are the watchers on the wall, then how do they get their night-watch reports to the elders at the gate? To whom do they report? With whom do they share sensitive impressions? Create a means for intercessors to have input. Seek their insights.

*Direct them.* If intercessors are "loose cannons," as some allege, it is usually because they have never been directed. Give them assignments for prayer. Let them adopt ministries of the church for which they will pray. Have every leader and worker enlist intercessors to pray for them regularly.[20]

Intercessors should model the spirit of prayer that is desired for the entire church. Don't allow intercessors to become an elite group of superspiritual types. True intercessors are humble and teachable. They often have a sharp sense of discernment and a deep level of conscientiousness. They want what is right! A servant spirit restrains those with a healthy prophetic bent.

Seasoned intercessors learn to carry, without becoming bitter and caustic, deep and often disturbing secrets shared by the Spirit. They are often the first to sense a storm coming and the last into the storm shelter out of concern for others. They are often the steadfast silent backbone of a strong and enduring congregation.

For those less mature, a teaming arrangement creates a natural mentoring venue by veteran intercessors. Don't hesitate to recommend cautions for younger intercessors. Encourage them to let a word from the Lord season before sharing it. Warn them against being a "spiritual bully." Caution them about using "thus saith the Lord" language so casually. Teach them to pray and leave results in the hand of God. Don't force a word or an action.

Intercessors major in truth; remind them that the greater truth is always love. We must speak truth in love if truth is to be life-giving. Avoid being judgmental. Don't expect everyone to pray like intercessors. Unite, don't divide. Heal, don't hurt. Fire always separates gold from dross. This kind of training will sift intercessors and reveal those with true hearts and noble motives.

Trust them. Listen to them. Appreciate them. Pray regularly for them. Intercessors come under attack, too. Gather them for fellowship. Protect them. Some red flags are cross-gender bonding, power plays, cliques, divisions, championing single-issue causes, playing the prophet, public posturing, investigative snooping, claiming representative privilege for another, more talk than prayer.

The end effect of intercession is reconciliation. The necessary warfare with the Evil One is only to establish peace in some believer's heart or home. Balance intercession with personal worship. Don't burn out. Don't spend all the time in the closet of intercession.[21] The heart of prayer is communion with God, but the edge of prayer is always mission. Prayer is first Godward, then outward. A balanced intercessor won't spend all of his or her prayer time in intercession. Time must be spent in simply loving the Lord. All prayer must be wrapped in thanksgiving; this keeps a portal open to God's presence.

Healthy intercessors can't live under unrelenting enemy fire. They too must practice the power of praise. Insist on balance in your intercessors. F. B. Meyer asks:

> What has become of so many thousands of our prayers? They were not deficient in earnestness; we uttered them with strong crying and tears. They were not deficient in perseverance; we offered them three times a day for years. They were not deficient in faith; for they have originated in hearts that have never for a moment doubted that God was, and that He was the rewarder of them that diligently sought Him. Still no answer has come. What is the history of these unanswered prayers? No praying breath is ever spent in vain. If you can believe for the blessings you ask, they are certainly yours. The goods are consigned, though not delivered; the blessing is labeled with your name, but not sent. The vision is yet for an appointed time; it will come and will not tarry. The black head may have become white, the bright eye dim, the loving heart impaired in its beating; but the answer must come at length. God will give the answer at the earliest moment consistent with the true well-being of the one He loves."[22]

When prayers make long voyages, they come back the richer, loaded with greater treasures. God gives liberal interest for the waiting interval.[23]

## 4. Prayer Evangelism

The fourth dimension to a local-church prayer ministry is prayer evangelism. The energy of prayer needs to be turned toward the community and the world. This is prayer evangelism.

*Pentecost and Passion.* Pentecostal pioneers saw themselves as living in "Acts 29." With the outpouring of the Spirit, the Holy One was confirming the Word with signs and wonders. Over the years something happened. Passionate Pentecostal praying disappeared in too many churches. Such prayer marked us as distinct from others. Now there is little difference between the typical Evangelical church and its Pentecostal neighbor.

First Corinthians 14 offers wise and practical advice for order in worship. Passionate prayer does not mean disorderly prayer or fleshly aberrations. Passionate prayer does not mean prayer that draws attention to oneself. It does not mean loud or physically demonstrable prayers. Nor does passionate prayer fear the intensity of voices lifted like a holy rumble as they cry out to God corporately. It does not fear tear-stained faces or deep throbs or sighs. It does not fear the searing silence that comes when an entire group is made speechless by a display of God's glory. Some argue that such an intense atmosphere is inappropriate on a Sunday morning with the church full of uninitiated seekers. Sadly, such moments rarely happen in any churchwide setting. Increasingly fewer intercessory groups pray with such passion.

*This Age and Passion.* Humans are passionate people. They are passionate about sports, hobbies, ecology, vacations, money, work, relationships, stamp-collecting, and Civil War memorabilia! But in many churches, emotions are to be checked at the doors of the church. That was not true among Pentecostals.

Passion is natural! The Evil One uses passion to his advantage. Half a century ago psychologist James Stewart declared that we live in a day when "spirit forces of passionate evil have been unleashed upon the earth." This is not a time for a "milk-and-water, passionless theology" or faith. We will accomplish little by "setting a tepid Christianity against scorching paganism. The thrust of the demonic has to be met with the fire of the divine."[24] Pentecostal faith with passionate Pentecostal praying is the antidote for the evils of this hour. Yet, we are shrinking back at a time when the atmosphere of our cities is swirling with crosswinds from the middle heaven. Our churches themselves are increasingly the victims of a spiritual stronghold.

> When the presence of Jesus is not manifest in the church in a tangible way and we continue our programs, we are inviting the religious spirit to set up her throne in our congregations and ministries. This spirit is more than happy to become a substitute for Jesus; in fact, it has been the goal of the enemy all along.[25]

"A lack of love for Christ is at the root of all that is wrong with the church today."[26] A loveless church is always a prayerless church; a praying church is likely to have people who are passionate about Jesus.

One pastor sensed that the Spirit was being quenched in his church. He canceled the Sunday night sermon and spoke briefly of his concerns. Then he asked the people to bow their heads and for those who felt he had quenched the Spirit to raise their hand. Nearly every hand went up. That night the service ran late as the people cleared their consciences toward God and one another. "The condition of the church may be accurately gauged by its prayer meetings. The prayer meeting is a 'grace-ometer,' and from it we see the amount of divine working among a people. If God is near a church, one of the first tokens of His absence will be slothfulness in prayer."[27]

Dwight Eisenhower rose to fame as a general in World War II. With much attention coming his way, loading him with accolades, he responded: "Humility must always be the portion of any man who receives acclaim earned in the blood of his follow-ers and the sacrifices of his friends."[28] We can never claim credit for the stunning victory that came out of the battle of Golgotha. The blood shed there was not our own. In view of His sacrifice, how can we not pray for those who don't know Him?

*Prayer Evangelism Ideas.* Here are some ways to heighten prayer evangelism:

1. Adopt the Moravian principle, "No one works, unless someone prays." Make prayer the essential to every effort. Anything not backed and bathed in prayer is human effort, which will not result in divine impact. Have every worker recruit a prayer support team.

2. Have church members create a list of family, friends, neighbors, and work associates who are not practicing a vital relationship with Christ. Ask them to focus on five names. Challenge them to spend just five minutes a day, five days a week, praying for those five people. After three months, suggest that they reassess the smaller list in view of the larger list. Give them permission to add to their list. Do the process over.

3. Celebrate the stories of open hearts, coincidental meetings, and unexpected connections. Remember, nothing is coincidental with God! Track His hand in response to prayer.

4. Create a "wailing wall" with the names or pictures of lost loved ones. Keep the fate of souls in front of the congregation.

5. Develop a neighborhood prayer strategy. Emphasize the prayer: care, share, and process.

6. Adopt a definitive subdivision around your church—a block, ten blocks, a square mile—or some specific geographic area.

7. Develop a spiritual mapping team. Have them collect data on everything within the determined boundaries. Study crime patterns. Get to know the business owners. Discover poten-tial collaborators (other churches and pastors). Pray for everything that moves in that zone—other churches, businesses, schools, clubs, bars, apartment complexes—everything. Be the change agent in your neighborhood. Put it on a map. Keep records.

8. Adopt community leaders for prayer—the city councilperson or commissioner, school board member, and so forth.

9. Pray for schools and firehouses near your church. Find out if special police units are assigned to your area. Introduce yourself. Offer to pray for them.

10. Prayer-walk the neighborhood—not once, but often. Systematically cruise your definitive mission area, praying as you go. Watch for changes.

11. Pray over homes for sale! Connect with new neighbors. Be the welcome wagon. Don't pressure, just be a good neighbor.

12. Monitor changes in the community—new subdivisions, new buildings, new businesses.

13. Do churchwide care campaigns. On hot days, pass out water; on cold days, pass out coffee. Set up a prayer tent. Do care projects in the city, but specifically in your mission zone. Give out food baskets to the needy. Look beyond the walls of the church for creative ways to care.

14. Evangelism means good news. Make the church a "good news" institution. Be good news to the poor and the helpless, the hurting and the hopeless, the unloved and the lonely. Be good news in the neighborhood.

15. Send prayer ambassador teams to nearby businesses with the message, "We're your neighbors at First Church. We want to introduce ourselves. We're praying for you." Jesus called us to be agents of peace in the community.

16. Focus on a high crime area in your city. Send prayer mission teams into the area to simply pray there. If safe, prayer-walk the area during the day. Look for measurable changes.

17. Pray for the peace of Jerusalem. Pray for peace-threatening issues in your city. Do this at least monthly.

18 Assign prayer teams to specific areas, businesses, issues. Sponsor on-site prayer gatherings of three to five Christians who meet at a given location once a week for ten to fifteen minutes of prayer. Mark the location of these consistent prayer-focus teams on your mission map and gather regular reports from them.

19. Pick at least two mission fields for which you will regularly pray: one some distance away and another nearby, but not in the area around your church. Move beyond prayer. Some mission fields are demographic, not geographic. Ask yourself, *Whom can we care for—widows, orphans, single families, the elderly, drug addicts, youth, gangs?* Prayer cares . . . and care opens the door for sharing Christ.

20. If your church is in a stable neighborhood, partner with a church in a depressed and socially challenged area. Help them determine a reasonable target area as a mission field. Stretch your own people beyond their comfort zone. Give the smaller, more challenged church the gift of prayer. Lend intercessory support. Send prayer mission teams. Assist them first with prayer evangelism, then with care impact strategies. Equip them to share the Gospel more effectively.

# Questions for Discussion

1. Discuss the relationship between prayer and the power of the Holy Spirit in Acts. Notice how often the church gathered for prayer.

2. Prayer not only changes the atmosphere with supernatural grace, it appears to change the nature of the believers themselves. Look at the character of the church in Acts.

3. Do you agree or disagree with this statement: "The fruit of the Spirit is as important to our witness as the fire of the Spirit." Are both supernatural? Are both fruit and fire essential for an "Acts church" witness?

4. Is the church today giving adequate witness to the resurrected Christ? Are you? What should our witness look like? Where does the boldness to witness come from?

5. What does it mean to be living in Acts 29?

6. Name four critical elements of a balanced prayer ministry. Ask yourself how your church is doing in each of these areas.

7. What are some practical steps you can take to bring prayer to the center of your church?

# CHAPTER 6

# Longing for a Great Awakening

**Foundation Study:** If God Came to Town

**Bible Focus:** Psalm 133

### Central Truth

God regards unity as one of the great evidences of healthy community and an essential to sustain revival. But unity is impossible without humility. Pride divides. It fractures. Unity attracts God's blessing. Psalm 133 invites an anointing on the priestly head, Aaron. This psalm is historic and prophetic. Christ is our High Priest (Heb. 8:1-2; 9:11-15). The Acts 2 anointing is the overflow from His coronation event. As the anointing ran down from His head, it flowed to His body, the Church. Acts 2 was the overflow of the acceptance of Christ in heaven's tabernacle. "He poured out this which you now see and hear" (v. 33).

### Key Principles

We see unity as a "nice thing." The very nature of our three-in-one God makes unity an essence of His very being. The kingdom of darkness is marked by division. Deference denotes the Trinity. A me-first attitude defines the kingdom of darkness. Christ humbles Himself, takes on the form of man, serves and embraces death. He does not seek to make a name for Himself, and gains a name that will one day make the universe breathless. The kingdom of the adversary is contentious by nature. There is no humility in that kingdom. There is at times a depreciation of self that still focuses on the self.

Getting others to serve self is the goal of this aberrant kingdom, whether by the imposition of power or helpless victimization. It thinks only of itself, first and finally.

Could it be that unity is not optional—that it is a critical necessity? Is the absence of unity in the church a sign of a greater need—the need for a baptism of humility? Where there is unity, God commands blessing. What level of dark power could stop the blessing of God from coming to a church or a community? If God commanded blessing, what could stop it? Is it possible that our problem is not the entrenched darkness, but our failure to qualify for the blessing of God?

## Points for Discussion

1. Do you see unity as a nice accessory or as a necessary essential?

2. Why would blessing be tied to unity? What does unity say about our character? About the nature of our congregations? About our relationships?

3. The Old Testament Tabernacle was a tent of "dwelling" for the presence of God. We are lively stones, fit together, and built into a habitation for God's presence (1 Peter 2:5). How does disunity and dissension affect God's tabernacle presence?

4. Mt. Hermon was a geographically distinct area. The psalmist sees it "socked in" with dew. The early morning fog was like a thick cloud that reduced visibility to near zero. The moist air permeated everything and touched everyone. Have you ever wondered what would happen if the Holy Spirit so enshrouded a city that His presence was inescapable, like fog? What if a convicting reality of God-consciousness invaded the streets of the city itself? What if no one or no place was beyond the impact and effect of the Spirit?

5. Not Aaron but Jesus is the High Priest of the Church. He was anointed to serve heaven's tabernacle. Pentecost was the overflow of heaven's coronation ceremony. The result was the impact on a city—Jerusalem. Thousands were saved. The movement it created was unstoppable. Could such a thing happen again? Was Jerusalem's revival a onetime event or a prototype of what God is willing and wanting to do in every city? Or both?

6. If God commanded a blessing for your church or city, what could stop such a blessing from breaking through? Is it possible that there are citywide, impacting blessings for which we have not qualified?

7. If community impact is our desire, and healthy community (lively stones fitted together) is necessary to invite God's empowering presence and sustain impact, how would we facilitate such community impact? There is no community without unity, and no unity without humility. Division fractures community. Pride drives division. Humility is the first step toward any sustainable revival. Humility facilitates unity, the ground on which healthy community is formed. Healthy community is the vessel into which God pours His glory.

8. What does a humble man or woman look like? What are the markings of a humble church?

## Insights

Revivals in churches are wonderful. But is it possible that God longs to send revival to whole cities? What would it look like to see a whole city experiencing an awakening? What would it be like to see a whole nation in a sovereignly orchestrated spiritual awakening?

# Such a Pleasant Place

It was Elijah's last day on the earth (2 Kings 2). Elisha refused to leave him. They journeyed from Gilgal to Bethel and back to Jericho. They crossed the Jordan River after it miraculously parted with Elijah's mantle. The sons of the prophets were in tow. Then, the chariot of fire swept down to the earth from another world, and Elijah was gone. Left behind was the symbol of his prophetic anointing—his mantle. Elisha clutched it as his own. He smote the Jordan and it parted again. The sons of the prophets gasped, "The spirit of Elijah rests on Elisha" (v. 15). Returning toward Jericho, the men of the city seized the moment. They needed a miracle for their town. They explained their dilemma. "This city is pleasant . . . but the water is bad, and the ground barren" (v. 19).

## Bad Water

If you have ever sipped fruit juice in balmy Jericho, you have to agree, it is "such a pleasant place." Yet, the water was not merely bad, it was deadly. Their children were dying due to the poison water. The toxic water was also destroying their harvest. There was no fruit. Despite its climate and charm, why would you call any place *pleasant* if your children were dying and there was no harvest? Unfortunately, we have just described America! It is "such a pleasant place."

Yet, our kids are dying. The spiritual water is killing them. We have not had a harvest in forty years. The rate of church closures is alarming. One-third of America's churches will close their doors within the next decade.[1] This infers that we are a nation that at one time knew God. Seventy percent of professed Christians are in survival mode, according to church analyst Lyle Schaller. Only 3 to 5 percent are in a "Kingdom-building mode."[2] A *U.S. News and World Report* cover story used this headline, "Cheating, Writing and Arithmetic: A New Epidemic of Fraud Is Sweeping Through Our Schools."[3] Eight thousand kids are contracting a sexually transmitted disease (STD) every day in America. One such STD is responsible for nearly 98 percent of all cervical cancers in the nation. We have sown to the wind and we are now in the midst of a deadly killer storm.[4] Pornography in America brings in $51 billion annually.[5] The church itself has been plagued by moral scandals. Less than half of the American population has "a lot of confidence" in the church.[6]

Those attending church are increasingly disappointed (48 percent) with their worship experience. The assessments include terms like "outdated," "just a performance," "boring," "disappointing," "embarrassing."[7] "Increasingly," George Barna notes, "faith commitment is viewed as a hobby rather than as a necessity for personal wholeness."[8] The late Bill Bright lamented:

> [The church] is asleep. Polluted with the desires and materialism of the world, she knows little about spiritual discipline and living the Spirit-filled life. She is complacent and at ease, thinking she has everything and is in need of nothing. [She is] a mirror image of the churches of Ephesus and Laodicea.[9]

Only 8 percent of Americans are atheist,[10] but they are more passionate in fighting something and Someone they say doesn't exist than the church is in standing for the resurrected Christ. DeMoss describes the current church in bleak terms:

> The floodgates of unholiness—including willful, presumptuous, blatant sin—have opened up within the church. Adultery, drunkenness, abuse, profanity, outbursts of temper, divorce, pornography, immodest dress—such sins among professing believers, often members in good standing of respected local churches, are no longer rare exceptions.
>
> And then there are the more "respectable" forms of sewage that are often overlooked and tolerated among believers—things like overspending, unpaid debts, gluttony, gossip, greed, covetousness, bitterness, pride, critical spirits, backbiting, temporal values, self-centeredness, and broken relationships. Sadly, the church—the place intended to showcase the glory and holiness of God—has become a safe place to sin.[11]

Witchcraft and cultic arts are flooding into society. The Harry Potter books have become a primer in public schools for induction of children into the dark spirit-world. It is viewed as a fictional fantasy by Americans, a harmless intellectual escape. From such journeys into darkness some do not return. Although 58 percent of Americans reject the existence of Satan, he is nevertheless real. He *does* lurk in the darkness. Israel was plagued by its temptation to flirt with dark spiritual powers, but it was always a costly departure from true faith. America is now being seduced. The preferred faith for our teens is now witchcraft. The church is keeping only 4 percent of its teens.

One in five Americans are now aligned with New Age belief systems, and some are active church members. The church itself is being shaped by New Age viewpoints. The journey within is replacing the yearning for the Most High God. Questions about the meaning of life and the universe itself, about the power of self and the potential for the paranormal are preoccupying young adults. "The result is that psychology has become the vehicle for an emerging form of religiousness."[12]

The psychologizing of faith in order to legitimize it and present it to society in a more palatable way assumes that in its original state it is unpresentable. This is a tragic tactical error on the part of the contemporary church. It is not "the faith" that needs to be reformed, it is *the church*.

## Breaking the Spell

William Bridges, in his classic book *Transitions*, says the difference between disillusionment and disenchantment is the key to change. Disillusionment, he says, causes us to recoil at defeat or failure, regroup and then try the same thing again. It causes pastors to move from one church to another only to repeat the same pattern. Parishioners hope a new pastor will lead them to the revival they have longed for. Both are disappointed.

*Disillusionment* will never fix the problem. Working with the same tool kit and the same mind-set, we are "enchanted" with the notion that we left out one component in the last strategic plan. So we do essentially the same thing again! With the same failed principles, we are destined to a similar dismal outcome. Disenchantment is different. It steps outside the systemic model in which we have thought and lived. It refuses to work with the same tired presuppositions. It throws off "the spell."

Spiritual warfare is an insidious thing. If it were tagged with Satan's initials clearly posted, it would be easier to combat. Among his most effective strategies are thinking patterns (2 Cor. 10:4-5) so commonly accepted that we fail to see the evil with which they are laced. Discernment fails when we are in denial and unwilling to consider the possibility that Satan's schemes and devices have imperceptibly infiltrated and influenced our own thinking.

What we have been doing for the last forty years has not been working. We are losing the whole culture. And it is happening "on our watch!" Einstein once said, "You cannot solve a problem with the same level of intelligence that created it." We have to step outside of our systems and consider new wineskins.

## Needed, a Fresh Vessel

Elisha asked the men of Jericho for a fresh, unused vessel and salt for the bitter water. A fresh, new vessel is often what God uses to bring a great awakening! He looks to men and women. He is now looking for a fresh vessel—a Jonathan Edwards, a David Brainerd, a Martin Luther, a William Seymour, a Richard Spurling—in this generation. Elisha asked to be taken to the source of the water in the city. Water is often used as a metaphor for the Spirit (Ps. 1:3; John 4:14; 7:37-39). He poured water into the the new vessel, then poured in salt, a purifier. God is looking for a new vessel, an agent of cultural purity.

# OUR NATIONAL SPIRITUAL HISTORY

Historically, there have been four great spiritual awakenings in America since the founding of the colonies. What historians call the *Great Awakening* occurred from the 1730s through the 1760s, and is generally thought to have been the primary motivation for the birth of American freedom. The *Second Great Awakening* occurred in the early 1800s. It is credited with giving impetus to the Abolition Movement that, along with the Civil War, outlawed slavery in America. The *Third Great Awakening* occurred in 1857-1858. It was a marketplace awakening. From the 1880s through the first decade of the 1900s, a Holiness revival gave rise to Pentecostal outpourings. The power of the Spirit working in the church made the twentieth century the greatest season of harvest since the apostolic launch of the church.

## The First Great Awakening

In the First Great Awakening, Jonathan Edwards became the fresh vessel of purity that God needed. He was a part of a movement of united prayer and pastoral covenants. He is best remembered for his message "Sinners in the Hands of an Angry God!" It is a politically incorrect sermon in any setting where sin abounds. Puritanism had declined. Godlessness, crime, and immorality were flooding the colonies. The situation was dire. In most cities, the decent feared leaving their homes at night. The streets were filled with muggers and thieves. Deism was flowering. In the culture "the worst vices prevailed . . . if any one condemned them, he was set down as a fool."[13]

With church rolls shrinking, ministers in New England adopted, a generation before, the "Halfway Covenant." It allowed people who made no profession of faith to have their children baptized. These youngsters grew up without godly disciplines and soon there were more of them than of genuinely professing believers in the church. "Halfway" converts eventually took Communion and entered the ministry, resulting in a passionless and misdirected church, powerless to change culture.[14] This spiritual decline was impacted by the so-called Enlightenment. Most believed, however, that only "united, earnest prayer could bring a divine outpouring" and save the colonies. Ministers began to call out to God in prayer, seeking His face, in order to lead the people into revival.[15] That's when God sent the first Great Awakening to America. Without it, this would no doubt be a very different nation.[16]

## Our National Beginnings

The Continental Congress convened from 1774 to 1777, and opened the sessions with prayer. Firsthand accounts of the event describe the delegates fervently in prayer, with tears streaming down their cheeks. John Adams wrote that "it was enough . . . to melt a heart of stone. God spoke to Congress . . . and it built our faith." One witness said, "Even the stern old Quakers had tears running down their cheeks."[17]

The most active members of the Constitutional Congress were not Jefferson or Franklin, well-known non-Christian secularists. Gouverneur Morris was the final man to sign the Constitution, an act of honor afforded by his peers. He spoke on the floor 173 times, more than anyone else. The handwriting of the document is his penmanship. Morris said, "Religion is the only solid basis of good morals. Therefore, education should teach the precepts of religion and the duties of man toward God."[18]

The second most active member of the Constitutional Congress was James Wilson. He declared, "Human law must rest its authority ultimately upon the authorship of that law which is divine . . . religion and law are twin sisters, they are friends, they are mutual assistants."[19] Alexander Hamilton, another signer, viewed what was happening in France—and what is happening now in this nation—with horror. "The attempt by the rulers of a nation (France) to destroy all religious opinion and to pervert a whole people to atheism is a phenomenon of profligacy (act of moral depravity). To establish atheism on the ruins of Christianity is to deprive mankind of its best consolations and most animating hopes and to make a gloomy desert of the universe."[20] Wonder what the founders would say today?

After the Revolutionary War, the nation again fell into moral decay. Ties with France brought a wave of anti-Christian influence. Voltaire boldly asserted, "Christianity will be forgotten in thirty years' time." Shockingly, Supreme Court Justice John Marshall suggested that "the church is too far gone ever to be redeemed." Christians on college campuses convened in secret to avoid persecution. There was an epidemic of alcoholism. In 1794, however, churches of nearly all denominations rallied to a call for united agreement in prayer. This sparked the Second Great Awakening.[21]

## The Second Great Awakening

During the Second Great Awakening, the camp meeting was a prominent vehicle for renewal. Rationalism had taken over colleges and universities. Godly professors were marginalized. Sceptics of the faith were enthroned as the enlightened. Christian students suffered as a growing minority. Higher education turned away from biblical roots. Infidelity was rampant and a ruin to families. The culture was characterized by "promiscuity, profanity, gambling, and drunkenness."[22] Doctrinal division and spiritual dullness plagued the churches. Prominent preachers were joined by lay leaders with white-hot hearts, as critical cultural change agents.[23]

Isaac Backus promoted the idea that "there is only one power on earth that commands the power of heaven—prayer."[24] He wrote "Pleas for Prayer for Revival of Religion." The pamphlet was distributed to churches of all denominations. The first Monday of every month became a day of prayer for national revival. The nation was mobilized to pray. In Kentucky, a four-day observance of the Lord's Supper provoked a revival. Three months later 20,000 showed up for a similar observance. Thousands were converted.[25] Youth were impacted. A new generation was claimed for God. Revival shook Yale College in 1802. The entire student body seemed destined to press into the kingdom of God. Nearly all the converts from the revival entered the ministry. Revival stopped scepticism in its tracks and returned the helm of the country to the godly."[26] The wild frontier, full of gambling and vice, was transformed. The lamb of Christianity tamed the roaring lion of sin. This turned "drunkards, horse thieves, gamblers, cock fighters, and murderers into evangelists."[27]

Logan County, Kentucky, had become a harbor for fugitives from the law. It was nicknamed Rogues' Harbor. Even there, after a Presbyterian minister named James McGready called three small congregations to solemn prayer, crowds ranging from 10,000 to 25,000 gathered for revivals. By January of 1801, these great camp meeting revivals were spreading from county to county in Kentucky and Tennessee. Eyewitnesses wrote, "The roads were crowded with wagons, carriages, horses and footmen moving to the solemn camp."

Several preachers would be preaching at different places in the camp at the same time. Hundreds of people would be "struck down" at the same time. They would remain still for as long as fifteen minutes, and some for as long as six to eight hours. At times the roar of people praying and crying out to God was like the sound of Niagara. People fell under the influence of a deep conviction "as if a battery of a thousand guns had been opened upon them."[28] Helpless, before God's presence, they wept. They repented and their lives were forever changed. New York congregations joined in prayer. An awakening swept through Long Island in 1799. Infidelity was swept away. Taverns were deserted. Family feuds gave way to brotherly love. Some denominations quadrupled during this period. The American Bible Society and the American Tract Society were born. A number of Christian magazines began publication. The American Sunday School Union was created. The YMCA was launched. Historians say the Awakening again saved the nation from French rationalism, greed and godlessness, and from frontier violence.[29]

## The Third Great Awakening

The Third Great Awakening is sometimes called the Layman's Prayer Revival. It began in New York (1857-1858) as a noontime prayer meeting. America needed a renewal. Crime was widespread. Banks were folding. The times were difficult and the church was again ineffective.[30] In the middle of a gold rush, gains grew in some sectors but godliness declined.

Jeremiah Lamphier felt the need for prayer. He promoted a businessmen's prayer meeting. Signs invited people to stop in for a few minutes. By 12:30, no one had showed up. Then Lamphier heard footsteps, first one and then another, until six had gathered for prayer. Twenty men came the next week, then forty. The weekly meeting became daily. And that week, on October 14, 1857, the nation had the greatest financial panic in history. Banks closed. Unemployment skyrocketed. Families were without food. Attendance at the prayer gathering swelled to more than 3,000. Every sector of society showed up and sat together, praying.[31] Soon, other prayer gatherings spread across the city, then across the nation. In six months, at least 10,000 businessmen were gathering in New York alone. Churches were full. Almost every public venue was crowded with people praying.

The Spirit of God settled on New York. Sinners came to the prayer meetings. Thousands became devoted followers of Christ. Crime and vice drastically declined. The wealthy generously helped the poor.

Ships coming into New York harbor came under the power of God's presence. On one ship, a captain and thirty men were converted to Christ before the ship docked. As sailors on one ship knelt for prayer, others mocked; but the power of God gripped them and they humbly knelt in repentance. By March 1858, from Maine to California, there was hardly a village or town to be found where a special "divine power" was not displayed.

- In Chicago, 2,000 men met at noon for prayer.
- In Philadelphia, 4,000 were meeting. "I have never, I think, been present at a more stirring and edifying prayer meeting . . . a divine influence seemed manifest . . . hearts melted," one person reported.
- In Waco, Texas, "Day and night the church has been crowded. . . . Never before have we seen a whole community so effectually under a religious influence . . . thoroughly regenerated."
- New Haven, Connecticut, newspaper reports, "City's Biggest Church Packed Daily for Prayer" and "Revival Sweeps Yale."
- In Bethel, Connecticut, "Business Shuts Down for an Hour Each Day—Everybody Prays." Headlines reported, "State Legislators Get Down on Knees."
- In Washington, D.C., the bold print read, "Five Prayer Meetings Go Round the Clock."[32]
- In Louisville, Kentucky, it was said, "The Spirit of God seems to be brooding over our city."

In cities across the nation, signs went up at noon, "Closed for Prayer!" The whole nation seemed to be stopping for prayer . . . and God touched the nation. Every morning, a call to prayer in the legislature of New York drew crowds. Boston's leading businessmen attended prayer meetings. One writer said, "Publicans and sinners are awakened, and are entering the prayer meetings of their own accord. Some of them manifest signs of sincere repentance."

It was estimated that 50,000 people a week were being converted. Church membership leaped. The numbers indicate that one of every thirty citizens in the whole nation was swept into the church by the revival.[33] Honor was restored. Any business that injured the community was regarded as wrong. People began to be more honest, truthful, and conscientious.

## Azusa Street

In 1906, revival came to a humble livery stable at 312 Azusa Street in Los Angeles. On the morning of the San Francisco earthquake, Los Angeles was also rolled out of bed. Folks grabbed the morning paper, but instead of news about the earthquake, the front page offered news about a different stirring: "Weird Babble of Tongues." It seemed the whole city wanted to investigate.

The meetings were held three times daily, at times for twenty-four hours a day. They cut across socioeconomic and racial barriers. Joel's prophecy was fulfilled again—there was a Pentecostal infusion of power into an anemic church. Yet, like the great revivals before it, repentance, humility, unity, prayer, waiting on God, and a hunger for holiness were at its heart. The Pentecostal revival quickly spread across the nation and around the world.

- Atlanta newspapers reported an amazing revival of prayer sweeping the city.

- The Supreme Court of Georgia, stores, factories, offices, and even saloons closed their doors so people could attend noon prayer meetings.

- In one small Kentucky town, a thousand people came to Christ in less than two months.

- In Atlantic City, only 50 unconverted adults remained out of a population of 50,000.

- For two hours at midday, Denver was under a spell. The markets were deserted. The entire city was bowing before the throne of heaven.

Whole cities were being impacted. On college campuses, God was stirring youth. Bible study groups doubled at Cornell. Two-thirds of the men at Northwestern University in Illinois enrolled in Bible classes. Two hundred men were converted at Trinity College (now Duke) in North Carolina. Only a couple dozen were left unsaved. God's people were praying.

The *Michigan Christian Advocate* said, "A great revival is sweeping the United States. . . . The Holy Spirit is convincing the people of sin, of righteousness and of judgment to come." Regularly held prayer services were charged with spiritual power. The *Baptist Home Mission Monthly* noted "a quickening of spiritual impulse and life in the churches and in our own educational institutions . . . a remarkable responsiveness to the presentation of the claims of Christ upon . . . men."

## Camp Creek

For two years, Pastor Richard Spurling prayed for revival. Nothing happened, but still he persisted. He longed for a revival that would transcend differences between Christians, that would champion unity for the noble cause of renewal. While grateful for the

Reformation, he felt that Luther had made a mistake by anchoring it more to truth than to love. He agreed that the church was deeply compromised. But he was praying for truth dipped in love. He wanted the hard edge of principle paired with a loving spirit of reconciliation.

A change was needed. Spurling broke with his Baptist flock and founded the Christian Union with eight members. His vision, rising out of the remote corner of Tennessee near the North Carolina and Georgia boundaries, was breathtaking. He envisioned a global movement of holiness folk, filled with love, not fight. God's church would emphasize intrinsic doctrines and assert the importance of Christian service. The ultimate objective was "to restore primitive Christianity and bring about the union of all denominations."[34] He longed for deeper blessings from God and supernatural enablement.

After ten more years of prayer, in 1896, revival came. Out of that revival, the denomination known as the Church of God was formed. With almost 40,000 churches, missions and preaching stations in 168 nations today, Spurling could have never guessed how God would answer his prayers. The late Charles Conn, historian, writes of the revival that launched the movement:

> In distant counties the plowing was stopped at midday; the churning was left sour in the crocks; the cows were milked while the sun was high; and the oxen were given hasty provender, and the wagons headed over the hills toward Camp Creek. . . . Great throngs crowded around the schoolhouse, teeming out into the nearby woods, the holiness people "prayed, and shouted, and exhorted until hundreds of hard sinners were converted." Besides the hundreds that were converted and filled with the Holy Ghost, many afflicted people were healed. The diseases and sicknesses that were cured . . . are said to be miraculous.[35]

The social moral influence was significant as well. "Lives that had been disorderly became upright; men who had been violent became meek; drunkards quit their drinking. . . . Holiness to them was not a utopian ideal, but a practical way of living made possible by a divine work of sanctification."[36]

Preachers full of the Spirit went forth telling the story. Awakenings became normal happenings as Pentecostals declared, "Jesus is alive!" with demonstrations of His life-giving power. Persecution could not slow the explosive growth. Common men with limited education preached from well-worn marked-up Bibles. Calloused knees and unflinching bold faith stood cities down. Resisters became members. The rowdy were humbled. The climate of the whole region was affected.

## NEEDED! ANOTHER GREAT AWAKENING

In the last hundred years, we have had significant national spiritual moments short of a great awakening. In the 1940s and 1950s we experienced the signs and wonders revival. In that same era, Billy Graham became a national phenomenon. The Pentecostal World Conference was also born at the turn of the half-century. Shortly after that, staid denominations began to feel the impact of Pentecost. By the 1960s and 1970s, every Christian denomination had been visited by the Charismatic Renewal. It has been almost thirty years since the fires of that renewal began to fade. The typical revival has a three-year life cycle, according to some renewal experts. A Great Awakening is a macro-revival, culture-wide and nation-impacting. They adjust the national moral and spiritual bearings for a generation, but their indirect impact is twice as long. Our nation is in trouble again. Nothing short of a Great Awakening can save the nation now. In 1787, Alexander Tyler, a Scottish historian, wrote:

A democracy is always temporary in nature; it simply cannot exist as a permanent form of government. The average age of the world's greatest civilizations from the beginning of history has been about 200 years. During those 200 years, these nations always progressed . . . *from bondage to spiritual faith; from spiritual faith to great courage; from courage to liberty; from liberty to abundance; from abundance to complacency; from complacency to apathy; from apathy to dependence; and from dependence back to bondage.*[37]

## Cultural Hostility Toward Faith

We are beyond complacency and apathy. Something has gone wrong. Much of the culture is hostile to the faith of our founding fathers. Too many today are at war with decent Christians and their values.

- Rabbi Leslie Gutterman was chosen to pray at the Providence, Rhode Island, public school graduation. The officials wanted a politically correct prayer, but the Rabbi made a "mistake." He said, "God" three times! There was a lawsuit, and the case went all the way to the Supreme Court. In a 5-4 verdict, they concluded that the prayer was coercive. A student, they said, hearing the word God might feel psychological pressure to conform to some religious or moral principle.[38] Incredible!

- Pastor Richard Parker was ready to pray the invocation at the Warren County, Virginia, Board of Supervisors. Just before he prayed, the county attorney whispered to him that the words "Lord" or "God" were permissible, but not to say "Jesus." The pastor refused to pray under such a restraint.

- A schoolteacher was ordered to store his personal Bible so it could not be seen by students. A whopping 237 books were removed from the classroom library because they referenced Christianity.[39]

- A Houston teacher tossed the Bibles of two students in the trash and marched them to the principal's office. He threatened to involve Child Protective Services in an attempt to prove some type of parental incompetence manifest by the students' possession and obvious love of the Bible.

- A ninth grader received the grade of zero on a research project. Her topic was "inappropriate." She wrote on the topic of Jesus"! Her teacher refused to allow a substitute project.

- In *Stein v. Oshinsky* (1962), and *Collins v. Chandler Unified School District* (1981), freedom of speech and the press was upheld for students unless their topic was religious. On that subject, the court ruled, constitutional free speech is not guaranteed. It was deemed unconstitutional.[40]

- In St. Louis, a student was caught and charged for "praying" over his lunch. Physically lifted from his seat and reprimanded in front of all, he was told to never pray at the school again.

- In *Ohio v. Whisner* (1976), the Board of Education was refused the right to use or refer to the word "God" in any official writing.[41]

- A New Jersey honor guard was fired for saying, "God bless you and this family" at a funeral service in a veteran's cemetery.

- A state employee in Minnesota was denied access to the parking lot because of two bumper stickers on his car. One said, "God is a loving and caring God." Another, "God defines marriage as a union between a man and a woman."

- In McKinney, Texas, a pastor was charged with violating zoning laws because he had couples in his home for prayer and Bible study. The same city allowed home gatherings.

Most of these extraordinary and outrageous attacks of faith were noted by Chuck Colson on his *Breakpoint* radio program. The Liberty Legal Institute of Texas has documented hundreds of similar religious freedom violations in our nation. On October 20, 2004, it presented the Senate Judiciary Subcommittee a fifty-one-page report titled "Examples of Religious Hostility in the Public Square." Laws proliferate in a lawless society. In fifty state legislatures and our federal Congress, we have introduced 170,000 new civil laws.[42] This is aside from local ordinances and legal codes enacted by county commissioners and city councils.

All our efforts to replace the moral lines of right and wrong, that should be drawn on the inner walls of people's hearts, are futile. Laws never restrain a godless people. Outside pressure never takes the place of internal restraint.

Moralist Alan Keyes reminds us, "What started out as separation of church and state has now been elevated into the separation of public life from morality."[43] It is a prescription for the complete breakdown of the culture. Arnold Toynbee, the great historian, says, "History teaches us that when a barbarian race confronts a sleeping culture, the barbarian always wins."[44]

## Dirty Vessels Without Salt

George Barna compared the lifestyles of Christians and non-Christians using 131 different measures of attitudes, behaviors, values, and beliefs. He found no visible differences between people of faith and nonbelievers.[45] The contemporary church is not salt and light.[46] We are having virtually no measurable community impact. William Penn declared at the time of our nation's founding, "Let men be good, and the government cannot be bad . . . but if men be bad, the government will never be good."[47] Penn and the other founders knew that wicked men don't obey righteous laws. Where is the clean vessel and salt to purify the well? Elijah needed both a fresh vessel and salt!

# CYCLES OF REVIVAL

When the prophets predicted the fall of Israel, no one believed them. How could the nation perish? But it happened. The American experiment has lasted for 250 years. In the same period, France has gone through seven constitutions. Like Israel, we believe this nation could never fall. Could it? Could this nation cease to be tolerant of the very faith its founders came here to practice—Christianity? Could persecution come here? Winston Churchill declared that England needed a supreme recovery of moral health and martial vigor. America is now in the same position. Like a ship taking on water, it is listing. It is guilty of the sins of other nations. It has lost the power of salt and light. Dr. Erwin W. Lutzer, pastor of Moody Church, admonishes:

> We cannot be inundated by worldly values and yet meet our responsibility of keeping society from decay. How can we do it if we ourselves are guilty of the same sins? We must be brought to our knees . . . and only then can God give us spiritual victories. The greatest need for the church today is believing in prayer.

Dr. J. Edwin Orr, a Christian historian who studied the impact of great revivals on culture, preached a day before he died, "Revival Is Like Judgment Day."[48] What we call "revival" involves manifestations that intrigue us, sensations that thrill us, and sermons that inspire us. True revival, however, is likely to plow up our fields and uproot our lives so that we dispel traces of sin and evidence of selfishness. True revival is likely to cause uncomfortable disclosures and call for unpleasant changes that create awkward transitions in lives we arrange for our own comfort. True revival will cost. True revival will kill us—and that is the only way revival will translate into lasting cultural impact. Spurgeon said, "Make much of the cross."[49] Genuine revival, he said, is always "a revival of holiness in which people weep uncontrollably, and worse." It involves "a terrible conviction of sin." There is no authentic revival without "tears of conviction and sorrow."[50] Brian Edwards wrote: "You cannot read far into the story of a revival without discovering that not only is prayer part of the inevitable result of an outpouring of the Spirit, but from a human standpoint, it is also the single most significant cause."[51]

Matthew Henry says, "When God intends great mercy for His people, the first thing He does is set them a-praying."[52] Pastor Yonggi Cho has written a book, *Prayer, the Key to Revival*. He should know. His praying church numbers close to 800,000 members. The average church member in America spends more time in a single day watching television than is spent in an entire week pursuing spiritual matters.[53]

R. A. Torrey offers a thundering reminder: "There have been revivals without much preaching, but there has never been a mighty revival without mighty prayer."[54] S. D. Gordon says, "You can do more than pray after you have prayed, but you cannot do more than pray until you have prayed. . . . Prayer is striking the winning blow . . . service is gathering up the results."[55]

# Sounds of Awakening

Could a Great Awakening happen again? Could whole cities be changed? Could it be happening in our time and we aren't noticing?

## Almolonga

Almolonga, a town in the Mayan highlands of Guatemala, was, according to George Otis, "idolatrous, inebriated and economically depressed. Burdened by fear and poverty, the people sought support in alcohol and a local idol named Maximon. Determined to fight back, a group of local intercessors got busy, crying out to God during evening prayer vigils."[56]

Every morning drunken men were found in the streets, still incapacitated from the night before. The city was full of domestic violence, with constant unrest and four jails that were always overcrowded. Churches and Christians were persecuted. Evangelists were sometimes run out of town. The consequence of intense and persistent prayer was incredible.

After five-hour prayer vigils involving spiritual declarations of freedom over the city, deliverance came. Ninety percent of the town's citizens came to Christ. They repudiated idolatry and the local economy began to flourish. Now churches fill the city, often in places where bars once flourished. Christian World News reported on June 10, 2005, that crime became so rare in the city of 18,000 that the jails are now closed and no longer needed.

Fields around the city have become amazingly fertile, and are nicknamed "America's Vegetable Garden." Five-pound beets and carrots larger than a man's arm have been grown. Cabbages as large as basketballs are a part of the 1,000 percent increase in agricultural productivity. The whole city—15,000 believers—gathered for prayer. They packed the main street and hung from balconies. A city in prayer became a city transformed![57] Could this happen in America?

## Cali, Colombia

Cali, Colmbia, was home to an infamous drug cartel. Seven hundred to a thousand tons of cocaine a year rolled out of the city to America and Europe. The cartel represented the most well-organized criminal effort in global history. Blood flowed daily from a dozen or more murders. Car bombs were common. Assassinations were ordered by the cartel and carried out with deadly diligence.

Every institution in the city was under the direct or indirect control of the cartel; banks, businesses, and politicians were on the police payroll. Pastors were divided. Attempts at united prayer had failed. In the midst of this chaos, Julio Ruibal and his wife, Ruth, called their congregation to "prayer, unity and holiness." Their efforts sparked the idea of a joint prayer event for the city.

They had optimistically hoped for a few thousand, but the desperate city sensed the need for prayer, and 25,000 people came. The mayor was present. "Cali belongs to Jesus Christ," he declared. The crowd stayed until 6 a.m. Forty-eight hours later, the daily newspaper headlined: "No Homicides!" It was a first. In the next few months, the cartel came unhinged. Almost 1,000 cartel-soft police officers were exposed and fired. Intercessors began to dream about cartel members themselves being arrested. Six weeks later the government launched a campaign against top cartel leaders. Helicopters buzzed the city. Police roadblocks were everywhere. In a short time, all seven cartel leaders were apprehended.

Such victories are rarely without a price. This battle was not merely moral and political. The cartel had been consulting a well-known and powerful medium who was known as "the Pythoness of Cali." Believers were in spiritual warfare. The cartel became aware of the prayer efforts, and a hit man took down Pastor Ruibal as he arrived for a pastors meeting. Ruth, his wife, recalls the crimson color of her husband's blood spilled on the sidewalk—a modern martyr. Julio's death forged a unity among the pastors that was needed. Two hundred pastors signed a covenant of unity. All-night prayer rallies began in earnest. More than 50,000 Christians attended these quarterly meetings. In some cases the facilities were provided free, with the condition that prayer be offered for the mayor and city leaders.

The atmosphere of the city began to change. Explosive church growth followed. Twenty-four-hour prayer was instituted. Megachurches emerged where fledgling fellowships had existed before. Many churches were forced to multiple services on Sunday. "There is a hunger for God everywhere. You can see it on buses, on the streets and in the cafes. Anywhere you go people are ready to talk."[58]

## Kiambu, Kenya

Just northwest of Nairobi, this little town was under the spiritual control of a local witch named Mama Jane. Relentless poverty kept people in constant need. Alcoholism kept them in bondage. Violence was common and streets were not safe after dark. A group of intercessors gathered to pray. What followed was a power encounter with Mama Jane. Intercession won. The witch's power over the city was broken.

Revival touched the whole community. Crime plummeted. Rape and murder ceased. The economy caught fresh wind. New buildings sprang up. The church that spearheaded the intercession grew to five thousand members. The city previously had no church larger than a hundred members. Now other churches are breaking through what had seemed a glass ceiling impeding congregational size.[59] Pastor Muthee says the whole city is grateful. They realize that the positive things happening in the city are traceable to the spiritual victories won by the prayers of the church.

## Could It Happen Again?

George Otis says that some three hundred cities around the world have experienced some level of community transformation traceable to unified prayer efforts by humble leaders who long to see God manifest, not simply in their churches, but in their cities. Five characteristics are common:

1. *Persevering leadership* (Neh. 6:1-16)
2. *Fervent, united prayer* (Jonah 3:5-10)
3. *Social reconciliation* (Matt. 5:23-24; 18:15-20)
4. *Public power encounters* (Acts 9:32-35)
5. *Diagnostic research/spiritual mapping* (Josh. 18:8-10).[60]

We see prayer from the perspective of our prayer closet or small prayer group. We hear our own weak and frail voice crying out for revival and renewal; and it is as if the Evil One whispers, "It is all in vain. You are all alone." From heaven's perspective, the view is so different. From there you and I are not alone. It is as if "the whole of Christendom, all devout Christians," are standing together,[61] petitioning heaven for a great awakening. We are not alone when we pray. Our voices join the thousands of others, perhaps millions, praying at the same time. Heaven has to hear such pleas. "God shapes the world by prayer!"[62]

Our prayers live on after we die. They continue to influence events on the earth. God remembers us by such prayers. He sets His heart on honoring the promise He made to us while we were on our knees.

> That man is the most immortal who has done the most and best praying. . . . The man of many and acceptable prayers has done the greatest service to the incoming generation. The prayers of God's saints strengthen the unborn generation against the desolating waves of sin and evil. Woe to the generations of sons . . . whose fathers have been too busy to pray.[63]

Let's flood heaven with fresh pleas for a great awakening in America. Let's prayer-walk every street in the nation. Let's rally 25 million intercessors to pray until a revival sweeps the 25-million unsaved, unchurched people into the kingdom of God. When revival comes . . .

> A passion for repentance sweeps across specific geographic areas. Many people who had been unaware of the supernatural become keenly aware of it. They are stopped during their jobs as their minds are gripped by a terror of wrongdoing . . . throwing all else aside, they desperately search for a way of salvation.[64]

Ezekiel saw a river breaking forth from the Temple (Ezek. 47). Flowing eastward, wherever the river went it became a healing stream. The river, lined with fruitful trees, flowed from Jerusalem to the Jordan valley and into the Dead Sea. When this happened, Ezekiel said, the sea would live. Fishermen would line its banks and fish would fill their nets.

What a vision! A river from the house of God, flowing to dead places, causing them to live. A life-giving force! Evangelists loading their boats with fresh disciples at places where no one had dared fish before!

Jesus reinforced this vision. In the midst of the water-pouring ceremony in the Temple, He cried out, "He who believes in Me . . . out of his heart will flow rivers of living water" (John 7:38). The source of the river is believers—not a place, not a building, but a people. You and I are the vessels God wants to use to send forth His Spirit and heal the land!

## The Evan Roberts Formula

Evan Roberts was the catalyst for the Great Welsh Revival. So powerful was the impact that crime dried up. Judges found themselves with empty courtrooms and policemen without calls. Bars closed. Illegitimate birthrates plunged. Language changed. A cultural purging took place without new legal codes. Welshmen who worked the mines and used mules to bring the ore out found themselves radically changed by the revival. With gentler dispositions and purer speech, the mules could no longer understand them and had to be retrained.

In six short months, 50,000 people were saved in Wales. Two million were swept into the kingdom in England. This revival was the driving force behind the Azusa Street awakening. What was the reason, the formula? Evan Roberts called for four simple changes in the lives of cold Christians. These are changes anyone can make:

1. Repent of every known sin. Be brutally honest. Hide nothing.
2. Stop every doubtful habit. Even if it is not sin, if it is a hindrance in any way, cease to allow place for it in your life.
3. Go public with your witness. It is not permissible to be an anonymous Christian. Be humble, but be bold. Be gentle,

but be forthright. Be public about your faith. Don't hide your identity with Jesus or your love for Him.

4. Follow the gentle promptings of the Holy Spirit. Dare to obey. Yield. Allow yourself to be an instrument. Trust your heart. Care not what others think, only seek the approval of God.

# VICTORY THROUGH PRAYER

On December 8, 1944, the phone rang in the office of the Third Army chaplain. On the other end was General George Patton. "How much praying is going on in the Third Army?" The chaplain couldn't provide a sound answer. The next question was more direct: "Do you have a good prayer for weather? We must do something about those rains if we are to win the war." The inclement weather had created a virtual stalemate.

Outside, a steady rain fell. Patton expected *him* to fix the problem? With prayer? The chaplain found no prayer for weather in his prayer books. He typed out a simple petition of seventy words. He handed the prayer to Patton, who read it and immediately ordered a quarter of a million copies printed and distributed to every soldier under his command.

The general seated himself and leaned back, toying with a pencil. Here is what he wrote:

Chaplain, I am a strong believer in prayer. There are three ways that men get what they want: by planning, by working, and by praying. Any great military operation takes careful planning or thinking. Then you must have well-trained troops to carry it out; that's working. But between the plan and the operation there is always an unknown. That unknown spells defeat or victory, success or failure. It is the reaction of the actors to the ordeal when it actually comes.

Some people call that getting the breaks; I call it God. God has His part, or margin in everything. This is where prayer comes in. Up to now, in the Third Army, God has been very good to us. We have never retreated; we have suffered no defeats, no famine, no epidemics. This is because a lot of people back home are praying for us. We were lucky in Africa, in Sicily, and in Italy, simply because people prayed. But we have to pray for ourselves, too.

A good soldier is not made merely by making him think and work. There is something in every soldier that goes deeper than thinking or working—it's his "guts." It is something that he has built in there; it is a world of truth and power that is higher than himself. Great living is not all output of thought and work. A man has to have intake as well. I don't know what you call it, but I call it religion, prayer, or God.[65]

If Patton was right, if prayer affects the circumstances that determine the outcome of wars, how can we win our present war—not against mortals, but against hell itself—without the whole army praying?

## Questions for Discussion

1. Discuss the difference between a revival and a great awakening.

2. How do we respond to society's cultural hostility to the faith, specifically against Jesus? How do we balance love and truth?

3. Nancy DeMoss says the church has become a safe place to sin. Do you agree or disagree? What happened to holiness?

4. With much of the church now holding the cultural view that morality is private, how do we enforce a corporate standard?

5. United prayer seems to have been a key to each Great Awakening. How could we foster "community wide" prayer gatherings aimed at a great awakening?

6. Can you imagine whole cities under the hand of God's convicting power? Cities stopping for prayer? Could a great awakening happen again? If so, how?

7. Discuss the Evan Roberts formula for a great awakening. Is it valid? Rate yourself in the four areas.

# Endnotes

## Chapter 1: Understanding Prayer

1 John Bunyan, "True Prayer," *The Contemporaries Meet the Classics on Prayer*, ed. Leonard Allen (West Monroe, LA: Howard, 2003) 15.

2 Henri Nouwen, "Resistance to Prayer," *The Contemporaries Meet the Classics on Prayer*, 151.

3 *http://www.quotegarden.com/prayer.html*

4 Ole Hallesby, *Prayer* (Minneapolis: Augsburg, 1931) 16.

5 Jonathan Edwards, "Vehement Longings After God," *The Contemporaries Meet the Classics on Prayer*, 99.

6 See Brother Lawrence, *The Practice of the Presence of God* (New York: Revell, 1958).

7 *http://www.intercessorsarise.org/html/prayer_movements.html*

8 George Barna, *The Index of Leading Spiritual Indicators*, (Nashville: Nelson, 1996) 23.

9 Herbert Lockyer, *All the Prayers of the Bible* (Grand Rapids: Zondervan, 1959) 192.

10 R. A. Torrey, "Hindrances to Prayer," *The Contemporaries Meet the Classics on Prayer*, 152-157.

## Chapter 2: Personal Prayer

1 Herbert Lockyer, *All the Prayers of the Bible* (Grand Rapids: Zondervan, 1959) 5.

2 Quoted in John Comper Gray, *The Biblical Museum*, v. 5 (London: Elliot Stock, 1878) 127.

3 Lockyer, 17.

4 Quoted by David Jeremiah at: *http://celebrationfumc. blogspot. com/200711/far-too-public-david-jeremiah.html*

5 Maurice A. Canney, *An Encyclopaedia of Religions* (New York: Dutton, 1921), 288.

6 Jonathan Edwards, *The Works of President Edwards* (Worcester: Thomas, 1809) 219.

7 Clyde Cranford, *Because We Love Him: Embracing a Life of Holiness* (Sisters, OR: Multnomah, 2002) 109.

8 Charles Spurgeon, *The Treasury of David* (Grand Rapids: Kregel, 2004) 26.

9 George Barna, *The Index of Leading Spiritual Indicators*, 61.

10 Martin Luther, "Luther's Way to Pray," The *Contemporaries Meet the Classics on Prayer*, ed. Leonard Allen (West Monroe, LA: Howard, 2003) 72-73.

11 Francis Paget, *The Spirit of Discipline, 2nd Ed.* (London: Longmans, Green, 1893) 71.

12 Lockyer, 133.

13 *http://www.prairievineyard.ca/quotes.htm*

14 Harry Emerson Fosdick, "The Problem of Moods," *The Contemporaries Meet the Classics on Prayer*, 160.

15 Quoted by Stephanya Portukalian at *http://ismileforyou. blogspot. com/2007/09.html*

16 Luther, "The Psalms as Prayer," *The Contemporaries Meet the Classics on Prayer*, 40.

17 *http://www.studylight.org/lex/grk/view.cgi?number =1568*

18 Walter Wangerin Jr. "The Psalm as a House," *The Contemporaries Meet the Classics on Prayer*, 42.

19 Luther, "Luther's Way to Pray," *The Contemporaries Meet the Classics on Prayer*, 72.

20 Fosdick, 162.

21 Fosdick, 163.

22 Robert Murray McCheyne, *From the Preacher's Heart* (Scotland: Christian Focus, 1995) 14.

23 *http://thinkexist.com/quotation/prayer_will_ make_a_man_cease_ from_sin-o _sin_ will/188755.html*

24 Cranford, 40.

25 Foster, "The Main Business of Life," *The Contemporaries Meet the Classics on Prayer*, 16.

26 Foster, 16.

27 Foster, 17.

28 Quote by R. A. Torrey, *http://www.gotothebible. com/HTML/Sermons/powerof prayer. html*

29 Gerald Heard, quoted by James S. Stewart, *A Faith to Proclaim* (New York: Charles Scribner's Sons, 1953) 76-77.

30 See Ron Phillips, *Vanquishing the Enemy* (Cleveland, TN: Pathway, 1997) 29.

31 *http://www.liftupusa.com/pquotes.htm*

32 Barna, 23.

33 Andrew Murray, "The Chief End of Prayer," *The Contemporaries Meet the Classics on Prayer*, 11.

34 Murray, 12.

35 Murray, 13

36 Foster, 11.

37 Lockyer, 78.

38 Cranford, 159.

39 Paget, 73.

## Chapter 3: Family Prayer

1 Herbert Lockyer, *All the Prayers of the Bible* (Grand Rapids: Zondervan, 1959) 20.

2 Quin Sherrer and Ruthanne Garlock, *Grandma, I Need Your Prayers* (Grand Rapids: Zondervan, 2002), 28-29.

3 "How Father's Faith is Crucial to Children's Faith," by Robbie Lowe. HYPERLINK *http://www.ad2000.com.au/articles/2003/oct2003p10 _1457. html*

4 *http://www.brfwitness.org/Articles/2002v37n1.htm*

5 Matthew Henry, quoted by Lockyer, 20.

6 Bill Hull, *Revival That Transforms,* 38.

7 Adapted from Clarence Shuler, *Your Wife Can Be Your Best Friend* (Chicago: Moody, 2000).

8 Tom Bisset, *Why Christian Kids Leave the Faith* (Grand Rapids: Discovery House, 1997) 205-207.

9 Sherrer and Garlock, 43.

10 Dale Evans with Carole C. Carlson, *Our Values* (Grand Rapids: Revell, 1997) 86.

## Chapter 4: Intercession and Evangelism

1 Quoted by P. Douglas Small, *Transforming Your Church Into a House of Prayer*, 103.

2 George Barna, *The Index of Leading Spiritual Indicators*, 77.

3 Barna, 106.

4 Susan Gaddis, *Intercessors: God's End-Time Vanguard* (Pathway Press: Cleveland, TN, 1999), 21.

5 Quoted by Bill Thrasher, *Victorious Praying* (Moody: Chicago, 2003), 41.

6 *http://www.christian-prayer-quotes.christian-attorney.net/*

7 Small, 103

8 Small, 103

9 Quoted in John R. Mott, *The Evangelization of the World in This Generation* (New York: SVM, 1900) 190.

10 Herbert Lockyer, *All the Prayers of the Bible* (Grand Rapids: Zondervan, 1959) 253.

11 Lockyer, 255.

12 Quoted by Griffin, *Firestorms of Revival* (Lake Mary, FL: Strang, 2006) 140.

13 Lockyer, 22.

14 Lockyer, 268.

15 Quoted by E. M. Bounds, *The Best of E. M. Bounds* (Grand Rapids: Baker, 1981) 55.

16 Lockyer, 221.

17 O Hallesby, *Prayer* (Minneapolis: Augsburg, 1931) 104.

18 Quoted by Alice Patterson, *http://www.unitedcaribbean.com/eagle-snest.html*

19 Patterson

20 E. M. Bounds, *The Classic Collection on Prayer* (Gainseville, FL: Bridge-Logos Publishers, 2001) 571-572.

## Chapter 5: The Ministry of Prayer in the Church

1 Quoted at *http://www.calvarysbd.com/quotes_prayer.htm*

2 E. M. Bounds, *The Best of E. M. Bounds* (Grand Rapids: Baker, 1981) 58.

3 Bounds, 61.

4 Bounds, 117.

5 Quoted by Bounds, 47.

6 Bounds, 47.

7 Bounds, 47.

8 Stephen Olford, *Heart-Cry for Revival* (Westwood, NJ: Revell, 1962) 68.

9 James Burns, *The Laws of Revival* (Wheaton, IL: World Wide, 1993) 54.

10 P. Douglas Small, *Transforming Your Church Into a House of Prayer* (Cleveland, TN: Pathway, 2006) 57-61.

11 See the Matrix Approach, Small, 64-68.

12 Charles Finney, "The Purpose of Public Prayer," *The Contemporaries Meet the Classics on Prayer*, ed. Leonard Allen (West Monroe, LA: Howard, 2003) 206.

13 Charles Swindoll, *So, You Want to Be Like Christ? Eight Essentials to Get You There* (Nashville: Nelson, 2005) 40.

14 Frank C. Laubach, *Prayer, the Mightiest Force in the World* (Westwood, NJ: Revell, 1946) 50.

15 George Buttrick, "Leading Public Prayer," *The Contemporaries Meet the Classics on Prayer*, 238.

16 Oswald Chambers, "The Key of the Greater Work," *The Contemporaries Meet the Classics on Prayer*, 257.

17 Herbert Lockyer, *All the Prayers of the Bible* (Grand Rapids: Zondervan, 1959) 25.

18 Small, 51.

19 For more information on instituting prayer, see the book and DVD series, *Transforming Your Church Into a House of Prayer*, by P. Douglas Small.

20 Small, 108-130.

21 Small, 123.

22 Quoted by Lockyer, 244-245.

23 Lockyer, 245.

24 James Stewart, *A Faith to Proclaim* (New York: Scribner's Sons, 1953) 102-103.

25 Rhonda Hughey, *Desperate for His Presence: God's Design to Transform Your Life and Your City* (Minneapolis: Bethany, 2004) 79.

26 Clyde Cranford, *Because We Love Him: Embracing a Life of Holiness* (Sisters, OR: Multnomah, 2002) 112.

27 Jim Cymbala, "Catching Fire," *The Contemporaries Meet the Classics on Prayer*, 212.

28 Swindoll, 138.

## Chapter 6: Longing for a Great Awakening

1 Bob Griffin, *Firestorms of Revival* (Lake Mary, FL: Strang, 2006) 23.

2 Griffin, 97.

3 "Cheating, Writing and Arithmetic: A New Epidemic of Fraud Is Sweeping Through Our Schools" *U.S. News and World Report*, Nov. 22, 1999.

4 Griffin, 234.

5 Griffin, 6.

6 George Barna, *The Index of Leading Spiritual Indicators*, 43.

7 Barna, 51.

8 Barna, 6.

9 Bill Bright, *The Coming Revival: America's Call to Fast, Pray, and 'Seek God's Face'* (Orlando: New Life, 1995) 19.

10 Barna, 10.

11 Quoted by Griffin, 26.

12 Barna, 28-29.

13 Henry Johnson, *Stories of Great Revivals* (London: The Religious Tract Society, 1906) 21-22.

14 *America's Great Revivals: The Story of Spiritual Revival in the United States, 1734-1899* (Minneapolis: Bethany, 2004) 6, 9.

15 Malcolm McDow and Alvin L. Reid, *Fire Fall: How God Has Shaped History Through Revivals* (Nashville: Broadman and Holman, 1997) 205.

16 Griffin, 110.

17 David Barton, ed. Bill Perkins, "America's Founding Fathers: Were they Christian?" *Steeling the Mind of America* (Green Forest, AR: New Leaf, 1997) 27.

18 Barton, 16.

19 Barton, 17.

20 Gleanings of David Barton, *http://www.christianparents.com/preserve.htm*

21 Dale A. Robbins, *Don't Give Up on America!* (Grass Valley, CA; Victorious, 1995). See also: *http://www.victorious.org/prayamer.htm*

22 McDow and Reid, 228.

23 Griffin, 111.

24 Mary Stewart Relfe, *Cure of All Ills* (Montgomery, AL: League of Prayer, 1988) 27.

25 Winkie Pratney, *Revival, Principles to Change the World* (Springfield, PA: Whitaker, 1983) 112-114.

26 Warren A. Chandler, *Great Revivals and the Great Republic* (Nashville: M.E., 1904) 189.

27 Relfe, 35.

28 *America's Great Revivals*, 41.

29 Griffin, 205; see also McDow and Reid, 247.

30 Griffin, 112.

31 *America's Great Revivals*, 55.

32 *America's Great Revivals*, 64.

33 *America's Great Revivals*, 68-69.

34 Charles W. Conn, *Like a Mighty Army* (Cleveland, TN: Pathway, 1955) 7.

35 Conn, 26-27.

36 Conn, 28.

37 Griffin, 29.

38 Barton, 18-19.

39 David Barton, *Keys to Good Government* (Aledo, TX: WallBuilder, 1994) 1.

40 Barton, 17.

41 Barton, 17.

42 Barton, "America's Founding Fathers," 16

43 Alan Keyes, "The Corruption of America's Freedom," *Steeling the Mind of America*, ed. Bill Perkins (Green Forest, AR: New Leaf, 1997) 40.

44 Barna, *The Index of Leading Spiritual Indicators*, 106.

45 Barna, *The Second Coming of the Church* (Nashville: Word, 1998) 6.

46 Barna, *The Frog in the Kettle* (Ventura: Regal, 1990) 138.

47 Barton, *Keys*, 2.

48 Henry Blackaby, *Holiness, God's Plan for Fullness of Life* (Nashville: Broadman, 2003) 3.

49 Clyde Cranford, *Because We Love Him: Embracing a Life of Holiness* (Sisters, OR: Multnomah, 2002) 113.

50 Griffin, 210.

51 Brian H. Edwards, *Revival! A People Saturated With God* (Durham, England: Evangelical, 1990) 73-74.

52 Edwards, 73.

53 Barna, "The Year's Most Intriguing Findings" (Barna Research Online, Dec. 17, 2001, *www.barna.org/FlexPage.aspx?Page=BarnaUpdate&BarnaUpdateID=84*).

54 Quoted by Griffin, 71.

55 Quoted in Dutch Sheets, *Intercessory Prayer* (Ventura: Regal, 2008) 23.

56 George Otis Jr., *Informed Intercession* (Ventura: Gospel Light, 1999) 18.

57 Otis Jr., 18-23.

58 Otis Jr., 37-47.

59 Otis Jr., 48.

60 Otis Jr., 56.

61 Martin Luther, "Luther's Way to Pray," *The Contemporaries Meet the Classics on Prayer* (West Monroe, LA: Howard, 2003) 74.

62 Bounds, *The Best of E. M. Bounds* (Grand Rapids: Baker, 1981) 75.

63 Bounds, 76.

64 James Burns, *The Laws of Revival* (Wheaton, IL: World Wide, 1993) 11.

65 The text of this article appeared in the October 6, 1971, issue of *The Review of the News*. See also: *http://www.thefreelibrary.com/the+true+story+of+the+Patton+Prayer%3a+the+author+of+General+ Patton%27s/*